IDENTITY
REVEALS
DESTINY

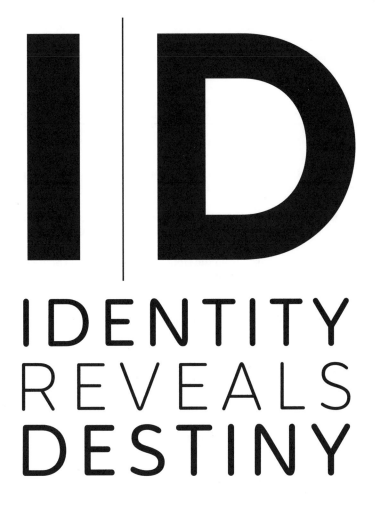

ID
IDENTITY
REVEALS
DESTINY

ALLAN KELSEY & BRAD STAHL

GATEWAY PRESS

ID Identity Reveals Destiny

ISBN English: 978-1-945529-58-0
ISBN English eBook: 978-1-945529-59-7
ISBN Spanish: 978-1-945529-60-3
ISBN Spanish eBook: 978-1-945529-61-0
Translations available in Portuguese, Chinese, and Hindi.

We hope you hear from the Holy Spirit and receive God's richest blessings from this book by Gateway Press. We want to provide the highest quality resources that take the messages, music, and media of Gateway Church to the world. For more information on other resources from Gateway Publishing, go to gatewaypublishing.com.

Gateway Press, an imprint of Gateway Publishing
700 Blessed Way
Southlake, Texas 76092
gatewaypublishing.com

18 19 20 21 22   9 8 7 6 5
Printed in the United States of America

Table of Contents

Acknowledgments

It takes two flints to make a fire.

—Louisa May Alcott

ID Identity Reveals Destiny is a dream that was only made possible by the incredible love and encouragement of so many. We are eternally grateful for your support.

To Gateway Church: It is such a blessing to call this place our home and our work. Thank you to Pastor Robert Morris and the leadership team for having the vision to empower people to find their purpose in life.

To the thousands of ID participants: Thank you for recognizing the God-given hunger inside you for *more*. We love seeing believers do what they were created to do!

To all the ID Coaches/Facilitators: Thank you for expressing your passion by helping others find theirs. We couldn't do this without you.

To Craig Dunnagan and John Andersen: Thank you for seeing the value of this material as a benefit to the international body of Christ. We are so grateful for the hard work of the Gateway Publishing team—Kathy Krenzien, Peyton Sepeda, Jenny Morgan, James Reid, Caleb Jobe, and Cady Claterbaugh.

To Pastor David Thompson: You took what was started and multiplied it. You are amazing! Thank you.

To our beautiful wives, Stephanie Kelsey and Dawn Stahl: Your love, determination, and prayer keep us on track. We are better men, pastors, and fathers because of you. We love you.

Allan Kelsey & Brad Stahl

Introduction

WHAT WILL ID DO FOR YOU?

Awaken Vision in You

Inside each and every one of us is a feeling that we ought to be doing or experiencing *more*. Even when we don't expect it, this feeling makes its way into our hearts, minds, and souls. Sometimes we dream about it, and sometimes this feeling unnerves us. It just won't go away. We say to ourselves, "Life must be different. There must be another focus for me. There must be another outcome."

We designed ID as a process to awaken this vision in you—to move it from an unconscious dream to an intentional decision to act. ID will help you identify the unique vision God has for your life. We want to encourage you and give you the tools you need to achieve God's mission as you follow His vision.

Give Permission to You

The ID process will assist you as you search for your God-inspired destiny. This statement may sound presumptuous, but most of ID is really a matter of telling people, "You have permission to search and follow." No one can stand between you and the dream God put within you. No one should dare.

We recognize that each person's road to discovery is different. We simply want to encourage you, guide you, and give you the permission you need to keep walking the path God has created for you.

Act as a Mirror for You

Answering God's deepest call on your life is more of a journey than a destination. This journey is one of personal discovery. God equipped you before you were born with specific abilities to make unique contributions to this world. These contributions are part of your identity. Discovering your full identity means finding God's plan for your purpose in life. Sometimes this can be difficult to see, so the ID process will act as a mirror, reflecting back to you what you may never have seen about yourself.

Provide Guidance for You

Many of us need guidance because we are often unsure where to go next. The ID process will not predict your future, but it will help you understand God's plan for your life. We want to share our experiences with you as we have done with thousands of other believers over the past several years. We know how it has helped us personally to understand God's calling and become aware of our own identities.

This process of finding your identity can be difficult at times. We want to make it easier for you. The Holy Spirit has led us to the ID method to help others find their purpose and calling, and we have used this process for many years. We will help you answer challenging questions and make critical decisions that will help you on your journey.

WHAT WILL ID NOT DO FOR YOU?

- ID will not help you find a job.
- ID will not help you see into the future.
- ID will not serve as a substitute for the voice of God in your life.

WHAT IS THE VISION FOR THE ID PROCESS?

Our desire is for the ID process to awaken God's direction and purpose in your life.

WHAT IS THE MISSION FOR THE ID PROCESS?

- We seek to identify people who are motivated to walk in the life mission God has given them.
- Second, we want to help them clarify their mission through the ID book and ID Seminars so that they will discover their genuine passions, talents/strengths, gifts, and God-given empowerment.
- Finally, we want to inspire them to continue their discovery by outlining a course of action and helping them choose an accountability partner.

WHAT IS THE ID PROCESS?

Our lives are often so busy that we shut out God's voice when He calls us to our destiny. New possessions or a new idea may keep us from feeling His call—a call to something more important in our lives. God calls us to more than our personal satisfaction, our success at work, or the approval of our parents. He calls us to something bigger than ourselves. In our private, quiet moments, such as driving alone in the car, lying in bed, or standing in the shower, we feel a gnawing inside, like a hunger.

This call is that deep, inner hunger. We all have it. We feel it more strongly at certain times, but it is always there. When we finally recognize it and think about it, the hunger seems so strong and affects so many parts of our lives that it threatens to overwhelm us. It may take more time and commitment than we have available for us to deal with it right now. We may ignore it as we fill our lives with more busyness, more possessions, or more information. Eventually, though, we cannot ignore it any longer. When we least expect it, something triggers those feelings again, reminding us there is something more important and more significant we should be doing. We just haven't found what it is yet.

The ID process will help you recognize that the real source of your inner hunger is God's personal calling on your life. We will provide you with tools to help you turn that hunger into productive service to Him. In finding your *identity*, you can discover and reach for your *destiny*. It does not matter how you came to realize you had this deep hunger or how long it took you to admit it. You may be unsure where to start, how long or difficult the journey will be, or what it will cost. We can assure you that the goal is worth the effort.

Are you ready to take the next steps? Admit the hunger is there and discover the vision God has for your future. Commit to action and take charge of your life's journey to complete the mission God designed just for you.

WHAT TOOLS WILL YOU NEED FOR THE JOURNEY?

To get the most out of this book, you will need some additional tools:

CliftonStrengths

Part of the ID process is identifying your talents/strengths. We recommend taking the CliftonStrengths assessment (formerly known as Clifton StrengthsFinders). To take this assessment, go to the website www.gallupstrengthscenter.com and click "Store." For the purposes of ID, we recommend purchasing the Top 5 CliftonStrengths Access. Pay the current fee, and you will receive access to the assessment. The assessment takes 30 minutes and provides immediate results.

(Please note: All 34 CliftonStrengths Access may be of interest to you but is not necessary for this class. Also, although we strongly endorse the

CliftonStrengths assessment, it is not required to participate in ID. If you wish, you may use other assessment tools, such as Myers-Briggs® or DiSC ®.)

Spiritual Gifts

You should also have your Spiritual Gifts test results available. This assessment is available free of charge through http://gatewaypeople.com/ministries/id/events/id-seminar. We highly recommend this analysis; the results have been verified and are used by Gateway Church.

THOUGHT 1

Admit There Is More

INESCAPABLE HUNGER

It creeps up on you at the most unusual times. Like a prowling cat that has been resting all day and is now ready to pounce on anything that moves, it sneaks up on you. These feelings and thoughts persist. They come and go, and yet the message never really changes. The constant tug always leaves you wondering about your future. You may have these feelings when you lie down to sleep, when you're driving in your car, when you're watching a sporting event, or even when you're listening to a Sunday sermon. The feelings are always the same. You experience them like a constant hunger, a sense that there is more for your life. This hunger leads you to believe you could and should be doing *more*—more to change the world around you and make it better. Deep down you know there is something you were made to do and that only you can do.

Busyness has become a normal condition of modern life, both at work and in our other activities. We may want to yell, "No more useless work! No more working to achieve someone else's dreams! No more work that keeps me from doing what God wants me to accomplish!" We may have agreed to pursue other people's goals because we don't have any of our own. Or perhaps we just aren't aware of our own dreams. Since we don't have our own goals, we don't have a plan, and making a plan seems too difficult. We give in to chasing other people's goals so that at least we have some focus. We are not passionate about the pursuit, and the feeling of *more*—that hunger—returns. This feeling reminds us again and again that we have no real passion for what we currently do.

Doing all this activity helps to pay the bills and may even make room for a new car or a bigger house. But how are we ever going to retire if we don't start saving something soon? The pressures of life make greater demands on our time and reduce our productivity. We live in fear that if we don't keep up the activity, there will not be enough to take care of our needs.

DO YOU REALLY NEED ID?

> *People are never more apathetic than when*
> *in the pursuit of another man's dreams.*
>
> —Simon Cooper

Do you find yourself less fulfilled by all the things that used to excite you? Many people's lives seem to follow this pattern. During young adulthood, we alternate between the playfulness of youth and the responsibilities of being an adult. We dream of an adult life filled with success or adventure—one in which we can make great changes or contributions to the world. Then, time after time, something takes our focus and interrupts our journey.

Somewhere along the way as we mature, we try to keep our dreams alive, but other things attract us. We turn our attention away from our calling, and something else grabs our curiosity. Before long, we forget all about our dream. Sometimes it seems we can almost remember it, but then it slips from our minds. It's like seeing an old friend from a distance. We walk away thinking, "I know we've met before, but I just can't remember her name." Did we really forget the dream? Or are we simply distracted by the noise around us? At some point, we realize our lives will end and there is less time left to do what is really important. It may be that we think we are growing old. Maybe the death of a loved one has caused us to consider our remaining time to live. We may be successful in our jobs but don't find satisfaction in them as we once did. Or perhaps we jump from job to job looking for something more fulfilling.

It is at times like these we wake up and finally realize we have settled for less than God planned for us. It seems like a false life. If you have reached this point, ID was designed for you. ID is for you if

- you have lost enthusiasm for your work.
- the most exciting part of your day is watching television or surfing the internet.
- you are excited when you see other people boldly following their dreams.
- you sense an urgency to get busy doing what God created you to do.

If you really wonder if ID for you, ask yourself, "Do I have an inner sense that I have greater potential and unrealized dreams?" If so, then ID *is* for you!

PERSONAL EXERCISE 1.1

Have you ever made the choice to follow someone else's dream instead of your own?   ☐ Yes ☐ No

If yes, why? Mark all appropriate boxes.

☐ My dream was not clear to me.

☐ It was easier to follow someone else's dream.

☐ I was not sure how to achieve my own dream.

☐ I was afraid to try to follow my dream.

☐ It seemed more valuable to follow another person's dream.

☐ I felt pressured by the expectations of relatives or friends.

☐ Other _____

PERSONAL EXERCISE 1.2

List three examples of things you have done to assist or help build another person's dream.

1. _____
2. _____
3. _____

PERSONAL EXERCISE 1.3

Take this test to see if you are ready for ID.

1. Do the activities of life in general seem less important?
   ☐ Yes ☐ No

2. Does your job satisfy you less than it once did?
   ☐ Yes ☐ No

3. Are you less satisfied with your possessions?
   ☐ Yes ☐ No

4. Are you willing to trade your success for more control in your life?
   ☐ Yes ☐ No

5. Are you escaping the hunger of your heart with drugs, alcohol, or entertainment?
   ☐ Yes ☐ No

6. Are you always looking for a new job and trying to find new direction?
   ☐ Yes ☐ No

7. Do you envy those who are doing something more meaningful?
   ☐ Yes ☐ No

8. Are you willing to change your life to address your inner hunger?
   ☐ Yes ☐ No

If your answers to these questions are mostly "Yes," then you are ready for ID.

Who is to blame for this endless search for fulfillment? Certainly, all of us must be responsible for our own choices, but other factors and people may have more influence than we realize. We will talk about these next.

DATA SMOG

David Shenk introduced the term "Data Smog" in his 1997 book of the same name. He explained how people are suffering from an overwhelming flood of data or information. Like the dense physical smog that hangs over large cities around the world, this flood of information obstructs our vision and clouds our minds. Shenk called this flood of information "Data Smog," and it can be every bit as toxic as the smog in Los Angeles or Beijing.

How bad is this problem? In the 1970s, the average person was exposed to 350 messages per day. By the year 2017, this number climbed to 4,000 and has continued to increase rapidly. Not only has the number of messages gotten bigger, but due to competition for our minds and the new mediums available, the messages have also become bolder, more dramatic, and more complex in order to capture our attention.

According to one study, the average home in the United States receives 11.25 hours of media each day. That is 11.25 hours of messages we invite into our homes, which should be places to recover and restore.

It feels as though we are in a fog we can't escape. When we try to run away, we often immerse ourselves in more media and messages. We drive home from work and listen to the radio. We arrive home and watch television. We catch up on emails and social media on the computer. All this information overwhelms us. Data Smog is now a documented medical condition that can affect a person's focus and well-being, create confusion, and hinder decision-making. It adds stress and anxiety to life.

This overwhelming flood of data may provide a partial reason for why we don't address the deeper hunger we feel. Every day, we feel a sense that something should be different, but then we take thousands of other messages into our brains. All this noise keeps us from filtering messages, deciding what's important and urgent, and creating a plan of action.

Allan: I experienced this flood of information when my wife, Stephanie, and I moved from South Africa to Lincoln, Nebraska, in 1996. Lincoln was not the most technologically advanced city in the world, but it seemed much more progressive than Johannesburg. Stephanie and I became involved in the church, school, and country club. We had accounts at banks and merchants. We went online to get information from websites and to keep in touch with our friends.

Soon I felt overwhelmed by the volume of communication I was receiving. Too many things were demanding my attention. I felt as though I couldn't give my full attention to my job or my family. At first, I tried to respond to every message I got, but it was causing a rift in my relationship with Stephanie. She felt ignored while I juggled all the communication that demanded my attention. Eventually, I just gave up. It felt as though I was trying to run a marathon by starting at the finish line and traveling backwards. Sooner or later, I would encounter the other runners traveling in the right direction. I would get buried by the volume of people, disrupt the race, and maybe be killed! So I learned to let it all go.

I felt so much better about spending more time with my family. But then I began to feel guilty about all the contacts, emails, and other communication that I was ignoring. I became more anxious and felt more stress. Data Smog still affected me.

Could it be that the enormous job of filtering thousands of messages and dealing with all that information, along with the other stresses of life, keeps us from the most important calling in a Christian's life? If we are not careful, we may allow the message from God to go into the trash bin along with the other messages we receive. But not all messages are the same.

God's call is the most important thing in our lives. He has put a purpose inside each of us that is unique, special, and life-giving. In His sovereignty, He sends us constant reminders until we finally recognize His voice as distinct from all the others.

This feeling of deep hunger is God's "message." It cannot be deleted. It holds the key to the purpose for which we were made. Listen for it; separate it from the Data Smog. Admit it is there and begin walking toward it. You can do this through the power of the Holy Spirit.

PERSONAL EXERCISE 1.4

Take a moment to sit quietly and think about your deepest inner hunger (your purpose). Even if you have ignored it for a very long time, look for it now.

1. Can you see it or feel it?
2. If so, how strong is its message?
3. Weak   1   2   3   4   5   Very Strong
4. In one sentence, describe what it is saying to you.

_____

_____

_____

This inner hunger is an invitation to your purpose.

MAKING GOOD CHOICES

When you become overwhelmed with information, making good choices feels much harder. The apostle Paul explains why we often struggle to make good choices:

And do not be conformed to this world, but be transformed by the renewing of your mind, that you may prove what *is* that good and acceptable and perfect will of God (Romans 12:2 NKJV).

Notice that Paul gives a hint about how the mind works and how to change it. Under your control, your mind can think one way with conviction, but with some intentional retraining, it can be transformed to think something different. The key is *intentional retraining*. How is the mind transformed? You must repeatedly expose it to the new ideas you want to embrace.

Think about a piece of steel, about as long as a measuring ruler. This piece of metal is made up of molecules arranged in such a way that they have no magnetism. Now take a very strong magnet and pull it across the piece of metal many times, moving from one end to the other. At first, nothing seems to change, but as you do this again and again, the molecules start to rearrange themselves. They begin to match the direction of the magnet so that the steel becomes magnetized. The more times you draw the magnet across the piece of metal, the more the steel becomes magnetized. This normal piece of metal is changed through the repeated exposure to the magnet. The steel becomes magnetized and begins acting like a magnet itself.

Your mind operates similarly. It is the product of messages you have received again and again. Some messages you heard as a child still influence you as an adult. The good news is you can transform your mind by renewing it. A mind is renewed by "washing" it with new instructions, thoughts, or ideas, just as you "renew" clothing by washing it with soap and water. You do this washing not just once but repeatedly until your mind is transformed, changed, or magnetized, just like the metal. These new instructions can be positive or negative; your mind will be renewed either way.

Do you ever wonder why you can't make good choices anymore? Your mind may have been renewed in the wrong way by the repeated messages (washing) your brain gets from the media every day. This flood of information is effectively molding your mind to conform to its ideals. The sad part is we sometimes make it worse by turning more messages on, looking for an escape from the brainwashing these messages caused in the first place. We come home feeling tired and wanting to hide from the world, so we curl up in front of the TV. We relax our brains and let our filters down because it has been such hard work keeping these barriers up all day. But then we let more information flood our brains. The devil uses these intentional media messages to support his three-part plan to *steal, kill, and destroy*:

"The thief comes only to steal and kill and destroy" (John 10:10).

Ask yourself, "Do the messages I receive every day lead me to be the kind of person I really want to be? Or am I like a piece of metal that's being changed or magnetized into something I shouldn't be?" A constant war rages between your highest purpose and your tendency to settle for less. In the end, you're no longer able to tell the difference between what is right or wrong, what is best or acceptable, and what is your highest purpose or simply the status quo.

With a weakened ability to make good choices, you find it hard to admit there's something more, and you stop trying to find it. The inner hunger you feel is God's call. He wants to awaken you to your true identity. He wants you to become all He has made you to be. Imagine what your life could be like if you were fully aware of your real purpose and understood that God has equipped you to do the work He planned for you before you were born. What would it be like to accomplish everything God intends to do through you? Imagine how you would influence the world with authority. If you are aware of this truth, then you can begin making the right choices. You can make distinctions in every opportunity and recognize when other things try to pull you away from God's plan.

PERSONAL EXERCISE 1.5

1. Write down messages that "magnetize" a person's thinking in a positive way (help them achieve a mission). Next, write down messages that affect a person's thinking in a negative way (hinder them from achieving a mission).

Positive	Negative

2. Circle the negative messages that have personally affected you.

3. Take the negative messages you have circled and rewrite them into positive messages. For example, if you heard someone say, "You are not talented," you might respond, "God has given me all the gifts I need to do what He wants me to do."

_____

_____

_____

_____

_____

_____

_____

_____

_____

_____

_____

TAKING STEPS FROM SALVATION TO LIFE MISSION

Step 1: Salvation

New believers go through a natural progression. It begins with salvation—acknowledgement that Jesus is Lord and Savior and a change of heart and mind about sin—and is followed by changes in behavior and attitude. Salvation is the first step in the process of becoming a follower of Jesus Christ.

Step 2: Life Development

Every leader has some kind of "wilderness experience": a difficult time through which God works to develop their lives. It has been said, "God loves you just the way you are, but He loves you too much to let you stay that way." While David was taking care of sheep in the wilderness, God was developing the heart of a worshipper, warrior, and king. As He did with David, God also wants to develop three things in every believer:

1. Character—so you can endure the pressure of your mission
2. Skill—so you can do the work of your mission
3. Heart—so you can embrace your mission with the proper perspective and priority

Step 3: Understanding God's Gifting

Next comes an understanding of God's gifting and how you should use these gifts to serve the people around you. It's a deeper awareness that God created you for more than just salvation. There is a real function and purpose for your contribution to the kingdom of God. This awareness usually springs from a deeper relationship with God and an understanding of the idea that God has something very specific He intends for you to contribute to the world around you.

Step 4: Beginning to Serve

As you become aware of needs, you begin to serve others by using your gifts. Although you may feel partially fulfilled, you still have a sense there is something even more specific you can do.

Step 5: Awareness of Life Mission

You begin to discover your specific life mission—the deep inner hunger that drives you toward what God has called you to be and do. The earlier steps of development are necessary, and each has a unique value and purpose in the growth of a believer. However, none seems to have the persistence of the mission to which God is calling you. The importance of God's call demands that you walk through all the other steps first.

You can't take shortcuts. You can't skip from Step 2 to Step 5! The length of time spent at each stage of development is unique for each person. Steps 1 through 4 prepare a stable foundation, supporting the movement toward the life mission stage with purpose, integrity, and single-mindedness.

ARE YOU FOLLOWING A GOD-INSPIRED MISSION?

Why should we be in such desperate haste to succeed and in such desperate enterprises? If a man does not keep pace with his companions, perhaps it is because he hears a different drummer. Let him step to the music which he hears, however measured or far away.
—Henry David Thoreau

Can you imagine being a musician without the ability to hear? That's what happened to Ludwig van Beethoven, one of the greatest composers of all time. His journey into silence began around the age of 26 as his hearing deteriorated. By 41, he could no longer publicly perform his masterpieces. By the time he was 44 years old, Beethoven was completely deaf. However, he continued to write music even as he lived in silence.

Beethoven's Ninth Symphony was the last complete symphony he composed. It's the symphony with the famous fourth movement, "Ode to Joy." Beethoven began composing it when he was 38 and finished when he was 44 (and deaf). According to one account, at the end of the premiere of his Ninth Symphony, someone had to turn him around to face the audience because he was unaware of their response. Beethoven began to weep, standing in silence, as he saw the exuberant applause of the crowd. He had just composed and co-conducted a symphony but could not hear the music. Or could he?

Beethoven could not hear the music the audience heard, but perhaps he heard in his mind something that no one else in the Kärntnertor Theater in Vienna heard that day in 1824. Perhaps the notes on the page resounded in his mind—just like a sound echoes in each of us as we listen.

God designed us to respond in our minds to certain mental and spiritual sounds. Many sounds bounce around us every day, but when we hear one that corresponds with the mission or purpose for which God created us, something begins to sing inside of us. All other sounds are silenced. There is a life mission—a purpose—for which God created you. It's ringing inside you. Can you hear it?

> As for us, we have this large crowd of witnesses around us. So then, let us rid ourselves of everything that gets in the way, and of the sin which holds on to us so tightly, and let us run with determination the race that lies before us (Hebrews 12:1 GNT).

God has given each of us a particular race to run. The word "particular" means that life missions are not all alike; they aren't created on an assembly line. God designed each of us with something *particular* in mind.

This verse from Hebrews also reminds us that our life mission is not the result of chance. Have you ever exchanged gifts at a party or on a holiday? Have you ever received a gift you did not like? Did you ever get one you really loved? If we're not careful, we can easily look at our lives and say, "I sure wish I had gotten something else. I don't like what I've been given." On the other hand, we might find ourselves saying, "Sure, I've got a great gift, but this nice life won't last forever. Life is just not that good, so someday it will probably be gone." The truth is God has given you something wonderful, and no one can take it away from you. Inside of you is a passionate purpose, a life mission worth living—just waiting for you to open it. The life mission God placed inside you is not a matter of luck or chance. God designed you and your life mission to be in harmony.

Hebrews 12:1 also mentions the "race that lies before us." God did not intend for it to be a mystery. Modern electronic devices are a mystery, and a husband and wife understanding each other is a mystery, but our life mission "lies before us." That means we can see it. It's not hidden or beyond our reach.

Have you seen your life mission, or does it still seem invisible? It works like a lighthouse that draws your heart in the right direction. If it is hard for you to see, keep reading because we are going to help you discover it.

PERSONAL EXERCISE 1.6

Is your life a harmonious expression of God's life mission for you? Or do you feel like you are being pressured, pushed, or pulled by some other force that may not be good? Below are five types of missions that might be influencing you. We have also left a space labeled "Other Mission" so you can identify any other mission type that is specific to you.

Consider the amount of pressure you feel from these mission types and label each as one of the following:

- Strong—This is a driving force in my life.
- Weak—It pressures my life sometimes.
- None—It never pressures my life.

1. Economic Mission
   The people who earn the money for a family usually feel this mission strongly. They feel the pressure to provide for themselves and their

families. The media and your friends often tell you, "You can have it all!" or "You deserve it!" These messages can lead you into economic bondage and a desire to work even harder to achieve a certain lifestyle. An economic mission is a seductive trap. Sometimes debt makes its pull even stronger. This mission can keep you bound to a focus that is not God's plan for you. "For the love of money is a root of all *kinds of* evil" (1 Timothy 6:10 NKJV).

2. Cultural Mission
    You may have a culturally-focused mission when you just do what seems normal for other people and don't pause to ask God what He wants in your life. You go along with society's activities and find yourself busy but with no real focus. A cultural mission may seem good. Society may value it, but it may not be what God has uniquely designed for you. It can keep you busy and focused, but it may not be the best focus. A culturally-focused mission can also try to limit you based on what society says is possible or acceptable. This deals with factors such as gender, age, race, or ethnicity. It wasn't long ago in American history that certain jobs were not available for people because of the color of their skin. Culture would not allow it. Do you deal with pressure from culture? Is it trying to shape your purpose?

3. Expected Mission
    This is the type of mission someone else placed on you. You have a strong urge to fulfill it because you think it's expected of you. A parent or spouse may have given you this mission. Perhaps you've experienced the pressure of a family business trying to reshape your life mission.

4. Other Mission:

Other than a God-ordained mission, what forces are pushing you to take a particular direction in your life?

5. God-ordained Mission

   Every person has a life mission designed by God. It asks for all your talent and ability and then requires you to cooperate with God to accomplish great things. This mission is God-focused, God-ordained, God-inspired, and God-led. You can only accomplish it with God's power. It invites you to work together with Him to do what you thought to be impossible. It's unique. It gives you power and frees you and the people around you to do what God has called you to do. It brings great joy, energy, freedom, and the opportunity to expand your talents and abilities.

> *The ability to simplify means to eliminate the unnecessary so that the necessary may speak.*
>
> —Hans Hofmann

PERSONAL EXERCISE 1.7

Which Scripture best describes your current condition?

1. "I have done my best in the race, I have run the full distance, and I have kept the faith" (2 Timothy 4:7–8 GNT).
2. "You were running a good race. Who cut in on you to keep you from obeying the truth? That kind of persuasion does not come from the one who calls you" (Galatians 5:7–8).

Is the second Bible passage how you want to be described? Explain your answer.

PERSONAL EXERCISE 1.8

Your life consists of many different roles, and each role has its own set of responsibilities. These responsibilities can be thought of as different "hats". Many times, we find ourselves wearing multiple "hats" as we try to meet the demands of all our roles.

List some of the roles you play in your daily life. For example, are you a spouse, parent, sibling, employee, coworker, community volunteer, etc.? Think about the different "hats" that come with each role.

You will notice blank #8 is already filled in for you: *Director of my life mission*. No one will care for this role like you will. Be sure to make time in your day for being the director of your life mission.

1. _____

2. _____

3. _____

4. _____

5. _____

6. _____

7. _____

8. *Director of my life mission*

PERSONAL EXERCISE 1.9

Now that you've named some of your roles, consider how you spend your time. How do your roles fill your day? How much time do you spend fulfilling each one? The empty circle below represents an average 24-hour period. Refer to the sample circle as a guide and divide your circle to reflect the amount of time required by each role.

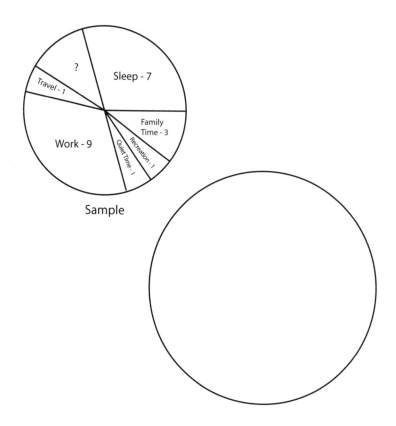

Sample

GROUP EXERCISE A

Answer the following questions and share your responses with a partner.

1. At what point(s) in your life did the number of roles you had to play at the same time change?

2. When did the value you placed on certain roles change?

3. When did you give more attention to certain roles?

4. Do you feel the amount of time spent on managing your life mission is adequate?

5. How could you change the way you spend your time to accommodate managing your life mission?

If you look at your life, you will see that you have had to adjust or change your focus at different times and for various reasons. We designed this exercise to help you identify where you are right now. Without knowing where you are, you can't accurately go toward your new destiny. The purpose of ID is to help you identify your mission and prepare to fulfill it. Focusing on your life mission may cause you to change your priorities. You may adjust how you value each of them or reconsider how much attention you give to them at different times in your life. During the ID process, we give you permission to turn off all thoughts that distract you from seeing your God-ordained mission. Focus on what God has prepared for you.

THOUGHT 2

Start with the Present

WHO AM I?

Answering this question could fill many books, but our goal is to help you address some specific and important issues.

CHARTING THE COURSE

If you have ever used a navigation software program (GPS), then you know you need two basic things in order to get directions. Actually, these are the same two things you need for charting a course on a physical map. You need a starting point (where you are now) and an ending point (where you want to go). With these two pieces of information, a software program will provide step-by-step directions for your journey. If you go past a turn, the program will tell you to turn around, or it may recalculate your route and give you a different course.

Unfortunately, real life does not work this way. It would be nice to get a message saying, "Stay in your current occupation for five years and then change to this job." But we cannot see the future—or even the path we are currently on—so accurately. One encouraging thought, though, is that no matter how lost we get or how many wrong turns we make, God is kind enough to reset our course. You're never so lost that you can't get back on track. Since we don't have a built-in GPS, we can use the exercises in ID to map our course. To do this, you'll need to identify where you are currently and where you want to go. Later we will examine the "Where do you want to go?" question as well as the people, events, and forces that influence our journey. For the moment, though, let's figure out where you are right now.

God blesses us with powerful tools to help us on our journey. First, He has given us His Holy Spirit to guide us (John 16:13). The Holy Spirit is like a built-in GPS for life. Of course, the ability to use His guidance and the power we receive from Him depend on how much we allow the Holy Spirit to work within us. Even an electronic GPS does not work if you don't turn on the power.

Second, believers are part of one body, the Church. God designed us to work together to achieve a goal or mission. Our membership in the body of Christ has several implications:

1. As a group, we have combined talents that make the whole (the Church) greater than the parts by themselves.
2. Since the Holy Spirit is at work in all the parts of the body, we have many people who can provide help and guidance.
3. We must work closely and honestly with the other members of the body to achieve the mission God has for us (Ephesians 4:25).
4. Each of these parts—every member of the body of Christ—also has a life mission planned in advance by God. We all have a part to play in acting out the great story of God's redemption of this broken world. This story will end in the unveiling of a new heaven and a new earth (Revelation 21:1–2). How wonderful it is to know the final result of the mission in advance!

PERSONAL EXERCISE 2.1

On a scale of 1 to 10, with 1 being most positive and 10 being least positive, rank your feelings of satisfaction right now concerning:

____ Your family life

____ Your occupation/job

____ Your education

____ Your physical health

____ Your emotional health

____ Your spiritual health

Now answer these questions:

1. Do I seek the guidance of the Holy Spirit in my life?
2. Am I in relationship with other believers?
3. Does God seem to be present in my family life?
4. Does God seem to be present in my workplace?
5. Do I eat and exercise properly?

Discuss these answers with a partner. How do your actions today reflect the way you rated your list?

IDENTITY CRISIS

God's mission for you as an individual is part of a larger mission for all believers. In many ways, Christianity is currently suffering its most serious crisis in history. It may be worse than the widespread persecution or the massacres believers faced in the early centuries of the Church. During those difficult times, the believers still knew who they were and what they believed. They were willing to pursue their mission, even if it cost them their lives.

How is the current crisis more severe? Today we lack the core thing that gave early Christians the courage to face death: *identity*. We have an *identity crisis*. At present, many believers no longer know who they are in Christ. They are not aware of, or perhaps do not accept, what God has done for them.

They know they are Christians because of Jesus' work on the cross, but they don't connect fully with God's redemption. As a result, they also do not make use of the amazing power available to them.

PERSONAL EXERCISE 2.2

Carefully read this list of promises God makes to believers. How many do you recognize, and how many do you live out as truth and reality each day?

- You are awarded more grace than you can exhaust in your life (Ephesians 4:7).
- You will do greater works than you saw Jesus do while He was still with us (John 14:12).
- All the things you break or have done wrong are hereby and forever forgiven (Ephesians 1:7).
- According to God, some of you will be apostles, some pastors and teachers, some prophets, and some evangelists (Ephesians 4:11–15).
- You were once darkness, but this is a gift of light. It is in you (Ephesians 5:8).
- This enemy will also be crushed under your feet (Romans 16:20).
- You are not only victorious in this life, but you are also more than a conqueror (Romans 8:37).
- You are handpicked by God to produce fruit and are appointed and equipped to do it (John 15:16).
- Everything you choose to do, no matter how difficult, can be accomplished by you because God strengthens you to do it (Philippians 4:13).

This is not a complete list, but it does show that God has promised us much more than most of us have accepted into our lives. These are gifts and resources God has already given to us, not simply nice things we will get in the future. The work is complete. God cannot give us any more inheritance than He already has. We must take hold of these gifts and use them.

If we used our gifts every day, we would accomplish so much more. The world would look quite different. Few Christians today take hold of them, which shows that we are not connected with God's purpose. We do not know who we are. This disconnectedness is the identity crisis of the Church.

Discovering our personal identity is a journey, not a destination. We don't get it from a short Bible study or from completing a course. We receive it by constantly moving toward God to understand more of who He is. As we become more like Him, we find more of our identity.

In order to discover your identity and truly answer the question "Who am I?", you need to ask yourself these two questions:

What Do I Value?

Knowing what you value helps to clarify who you are. Look at your life and the things you consider important.

- Do you value your car more than your children?
- Do you value your cell phone more than your spouse?
- Do you value your job or income more than your relationships?
- Do you value your possessions more than your friends?

Some of these questions may seem silly—because they are. You know the correct answers. But do you have an odd feeling when you read them? Are there other, similar questions that could also make you feel uncomfortable?

What do you value?

When you answer this question, you will also find where you spend your time. Jesus says, "For where your treasure is, there your heart will be also" (Matthew 6:21). Where you spend your time is a large part of your identity. Don't just be "busy"; spend your time intentionally.

What Are My Goals?

Having short-term and long-term goals will help you focus and let you know when you are successful and when you fail. They will keep you on track. Goals give you a way to measure your actions and encourage you to keep "pressing toward the prize" (Philippians 3:14).

PERSONAL EXERCISE 2.3

What are some of your most important goals? Consider personal, professional, and other life goals. They can be short-term or long-term. Think about one thing you can do to answer the deep hunger inside of you. Discuss your answers with a partner.

_____

_____

_____

_____

_____

_____

_____

_____

_____

_____

_____

THOUGHT 3

Make Peace with Your Past

As a single footstep will not make a path on the earth,
so a single thought will not make a pathway in the mind.
To make a deep physical path, we walk again and again.
To make a deep mental path, we must think over and
over the kind of thoughts we wish to dominate our lives.

—Henry David Thoreau

DEALING WITH THE PAST

If your journey leads from where you are today to your destination in the future, why do you need to look at the past? This is a great question.

Look at your past and where you are now. Consider both the good and bad influences that brought you to this point. Is it possible that things from your past are distorting your vision of the future? While God made us a certain way, the people we meet and the circumstances we encounter strongly influence our decisions and the way we live.

We all have our own perspectives of the world. In the same way that glasses shape the way your eyes see, your unique past shapes the way you experience both the present and the future. The past affects how we think, feel, and act, for both good and bad.

For example, if you had a scary experience with a dog when you were young, you may always be nervous around dogs as an adult, even if the other dogs you meet are gentle. You could be the kind of person who is easily scared. A surprising number of adults are afraid of clowns and butterflies, even though these are not "scary" things. On the other hand, if your experiences growing up were mostly pleasant, you may be a very optimistic person with very few fears.

Past fears can bind us emotionally and affect the choices we make. You may "know" you are safe if you don't travel beyond certain limits. As a child, you probably learned it is safe to watch lions at the zoo as long as you remain behind the thick glass. You know that venturing into the lion exhibit would be going beyond your safety limit. How many dreams or goals do we see as lions—okay to look at from a distance but too "dangerous" to actually engage? Perhaps you did try to achieve a dream, but your failed attempt was embarrassing or painful. This experience has shaped your perspective that trying is too dangerous and it's much better to stay on the safe side of the glass.

What goals or dreams are you not achieving because you are chained to your perspective of the past?

Brad: While Allan grew up in South Africa, I grew up in Southwest Michigan on eighty acres in the country, along with three brothers and three sisters. We learned to be creative in what we did for enjoyment, and with three brothers, we could get into a lot of trouble. We had a typical big farm dog named "Blacky," who stayed chained to his old wooden doghouse.

There was a perfect circular path worn into the grass around the doghouse. Blacky's barrier had about a four-meter (or twelve-foot) radius, which he created as he patrolled his territory, chasing anything or anyone who came near. That worn circle was a marker to everyone who passed by. If you wanted to stay safe, you stayed outside Blacky's circle.

Blacky had limitations as to how far he could go because his chain held him back. Even the other children knew how far he could go. Through their frequent visits, they wore a bike path in the grass about one meter outside Blacky's circle. They understood his limitations and were careful to stay beyond his reach. As they rode by on their path, Blacky would strain as far as his chain would allow, barking and wishing he could stretch just a little farther. It didn't matter how far he wanted to go, though; unless something changed, he was limited. Have you ever felt like that? Have you ever wanted something that always seemed just beyond your reach?

One day, I had the bright idea of moving Blacky's dog house three feet in the direction of the bike path. When the other children rode into the yard, they would get a little surprise! Only Blacky and I knew his circle had mysteriously expanded.

You guessed it—my plan worked beautifully! The children rode by, and Blacky barked. Only this time, he ran and grabbed one of the boy's pant legs and flipped him off his bike. Blacky trotted back to his doghouse with a sense of accomplishment while the neighbor boy lay on the ground in shock and confusion. I grinned, even though I probably should have gotten in trouble.

The same thing happens to you. Dreams ride by, but they always seem outside your reach because of the "chains" that hold you back. After a few unsuccessful attempts, we quit trying. Instead of dealing with the things holding us back, we come to the conclusion that dreams are only for lucky people, and we must not be lucky. We develop a wrong perspective and accept the limitation as fact.

Your journey is influenced by the people, events, and experiences you encounter. Let's look at some "influencers" who have shaped your perspective about life.

Family Members

Have your relatives helped you identify and develop your talents? Do they encourage you to find your own path in life? Or have they only told you to do what other family members have done? How have your relatives' words and actions influenced your opinions about the Church or social issues? How do you respond to what they say or do?

Teachers

Teachers play a significant role in our development because they have access to our minds at an early age. Their status as authority figures gives them influence, which parents and others in our community endorse. But there are two sides to this influence.

Some teachers and coaches encourage and develop great ideas and accomplishments in their students. However, others can instruct students in a worldview of which parents might not approve. Sometimes this instruction comes from the authority of the school or from the government as it imposes certain programs. Teachers are just like all people. They may have good or evil intentions. They may have to teach from textbooks approved by the state. Parents need to guide their children and work with teachers and schools to ensure there is a balanced approach to education.

What perspectives do you have today that started because of something a teacher said to or modeled for you? Is it something that encouraged you or set you on the wrong path? Do you have a worldview formed by what you learned in school? How has this worldview changed as you've matured?

Mentors

In many ways, mentors are like teachers, but they can have even more influence on us because we choose to engage with them. We seek them out because they do something well, and we willingly let them influence us. They may be more compatible with our existing perspectives. This can be a positive relationship because we are more likely to find mentors who are right for us.

We may have mentors in business, academic, or social organizations. They strongly influence how we see the world. Think about the mentors you have had. How has your experience with each mentor affected your perspective or your personal development? Are your ideas yours or theirs?

Other People

What influences have other people had on you? How have you been shaped by these interactions? Do other people generally encourage you, or do they leave you doubting yourself and your contribution to the world?

Events and Experiences

Countless events and experiences help shape our lives. Some experiences leave us stronger than we were before. Others leave us scarred, weaker, or more afraid. Our reactions to circumstances directly affect our perspective on life. For example, if someone is married for 15 years and then goes through an ugly divorce, he will likely have a changed perspective on marriage. The divorce may make him quite cynical, or with support from friends and relatives, he can learn from it and grow as a person.

Here is another example: A soldier lined up next to the men he had shared life with for 18 months. "Soldiers," the commanding officer said. "Half of you will be deployed to fight overseas after this meeting. The other half will become office staff around the country. Count off 'one' and 'two.' Now, all the 'ones' come over here. You will be getting office jobs. The rest of you: pack your bags. You'll be leaving for war overseas tomorrow morning."

This scene would have made some soldiers wish for a different result. Some may have wanted to fight in the war but were sent to desk jobs. Others may have preferred to get desk jobs rather than risk their lives. Either way, if we don't get what we want, it is easy to blame the circumstance. "If only I was a 'one' and not a 'two.'" "If only I had gotten into 'X' university instead of 'Y' university or taken another job instead of the one I have."

Circumstances can provide good opportunities, but they can also create perspectives of fear based upon regret. The apostle Paul gives his response to this type of situation: "I have learned to be content whatever the circumstances" (Philippians 4:11). What past events or experiences have affected your perspective of the world, whether in encouraging or discouraging ways? How do you respond to Paul's teaching about circumstances?

Personal Hopes

Hope deferred makes the heart sick,
> but a longing fulfilled is a tree of life" (Proverbs 13:12).

Brad: When I was growing up, I really wanted an off-road motorcycle to ride on Sunday afternoons. I dreamed about it. I asked for it. I hoped for it. It never came. Eventually, I stopped dreaming. Thirty years later, I still find myself staring longingly at a muddy motorcycle being carried in the back of a pick-up truck. I remember how much I wanted it and hoped for it. I remember thinking how much fun it would be to ride and even how the burning gasoline would smell.

But when we are driving, my wife never notices a dirt bike in the back of a truck as it passes by. That's because it's not my wife's perspective; it was not her dream. I notice things that she doesn't.

What things have you hoped for and received—or not received—that changed the way you see life? Do those hopes affect how you see the world today?

TRACKS AND FOSSILS

In nature, traces of history exist in the form of tracks and fossils. Tracks are short-term impressions left behind by something moving, such as an animal. They are easy to erase and soon disappear completely.

Maybe you've seen a movie or television show that depicted trackers—people who can look at footprints and identify which animal made them, how many animals were in the group, when they passed by, and where they were going. Tracks are fragile, so they are only good if they are relatively new and continue for some distance. Otherwise, it's easy to lose the trail of the animal.

Fossils, on the other hand, are formed in stone when part of an animal or plant is preserved after it dies and decays. There are fossils of dinosaurs, for example. These creatures have been extinct for a long time, yet their existence has remained visible in stone. One fossil can tell a story for a long, long time.

Can you see the imprints made in your life by people and events from your past? Some leave tracks—short-term impressions you had to see right away. These may be statements or actions that happened a single time. They might have been for good or for bad, but you remember and replay them in your mind and heart, perhaps for years. If they were positive, they encourage you and help you move forward. If they were negative, they may still be chains holding you back. Some imprints are fossils that develop and harden in you over a long period of time.

Brad: Growing up, I heard two voices in my head. They were trying to create an imprint. One voice would say, "You're just a dumb country kid. You'll never amount to anything." Repeatedly, it would play in my head. "You're just a dumb country kid. You'll never amount to anything."

When I would daydream about what I wanted to be when I grew up, I would hear it: "You're just a dumb country kid. You'll never amount to anything." When teachers would ask for someone to try to solve a problem, I'd hear, "Don't try it; you're just a dumb country kid." Any time I would make a mistake, the voice would say, "I told you not to try; you're just a dumb country kid. You'll never amount to anything."

Each time this damaging lie would play in my mind, it was attempting to chain me to a perspective—to limit me and hold me back from everything I could do. The more I listened to and obeyed it, the deeper and more visible the "track" became. This lie was becoming a fossil—something permanent.

The other voice was different. It was my mother's voice saying, "Why not me?" Three simple words echoed in my head: "Why not me?"

This was my mom's way of saying, "Why not try this? It never hurts to try something that seems impossible. Why should success only be for other people? Why not me?"

My mom always wanted to help people. One day, she decided to help people through writing. She told her friends, "I'm going to write short stories." They laughed at her and said, "Who do you think you are? You don't know how to write." But she would reply, "Why *not* me? Somebody has to write. So, why not *me*?"

She enrolled in a writing class that operated through the mail—a correspondence course. This brought even more ridicule from friends and family. "You're going to learn how to write through a correspondence course?" But she wanted to write. "Why not *me*?" She wrote several short stories and sent them to publishers. Being rejected, she began the cycle of rewriting the stories, resending them to publishers, and being rejected again. Finally, my mom sold her first short story. After writing and selling several short stories and magazine articles, she decided to write a book. Again, her friends and family argued, "Who do you think you are? You can't write books!" But my mother said to herself, "Why not? Why not me? Somebody has to write books. Why can't it be me? Why not *me*?"

The whole cycle started again—writing classes through a correspondence course, writing a book manuscript, sending it to publishers, being rejected, rewriting, resubmitting, more rejection ... Again and again, for years, she wrote. "Why not me? Why not *me*?"

Then, after years of being rejected by publishers, my mom sold her first book. Then she sold a second and then a third. Before she died, publishing companies were begging her to write books for them. In all, 96 books were published. Some were translated into several languages. At one point in her writing career, she was a top female writer of Christian fiction. "Why not *me*?" Mom answered that question!

I still hear her words today. "Why not *me*?" I have not heard the voice about being a "dumb country kid" for a very long time. "Why not *me*?" created a good fossil inside; those words liberated me to dream and try things that might seem impossible.

One thing is certain: our lives have imprints from the people we meet. Some have been good, and others have been harmful. Some have been tracks, easy to wipe away, while others have been fossils—hard, deep impressions that seem impossible to change.

GROUP EXERCISE B

Identify some of the imprints different influencers have created in your life. These imprints can show up in your mannerisms, your responses to situations, your beliefs, your decision-making process, and how you relate to other people.

Next, place a "T" to the left of the imprint if it is a track or an "F" if it is a fossil. When you finish, share your results with a partner. Ask if they recognize any other imprints in you, especially if they have known you for a long time.

- Relatives
  Good: _____
  Bad: _____

- Teachers
  Good: _____
  Bad: _____

- Mentors
  Good: _____
  Bad: _____

- Other People
  Good: _____
  Bad: _____

- Events and Experiences
  Good: _____
  Bad: _____

- Personal Hopes

  Good: _____

  Bad: _____

YOUR REACTION TO THE INFLUENCERS

In order to move forward with confidence, you must be free from the binding influences of the past. As we have seen, negative people, events, and circumstances can all play a role in keeping us from becoming what God wants us to be.

Next, we will look at the influencers you identified. You may not be able to change an event, alter someone's words, or erase your experience. The past is the past. However, you don't have to allow negative influencers to hold you back any longer.

Look again at your answers about the imprints influencers have made in your life. Think about your reactions to them and ask yourself these questions: Are your responses intentional, or do you make them without thinking? Have your reactions moved you toward your goals and God's calling, or do they leave you feeling like a victim of circumstances—even though you aren't?

Choose to Change

To make peace with the past, you may have to wipe away some tracks and break up some fossils. What follows are three ways to help bring about change. Decide which one is the correct action to take for the tracks and fossils in your life.

Let It Go—Forgive

Some imprints were caused by someone sinning against you. Forgiving does not mean saying others were right; it just helps you let go of what they did and leave it to God. Break word curses spoken over you by choosing forgiveness.

- Forgive others for ignorance. Sometimes people do the best they can, but their best is far short of God's best.
- Forgive others for iniquity. Sometimes people do wrong things because that is what they learned from their own past.
- Forgive others for intimidation. Their fears held them captive, so they held others (including you) captive too.

Change Your Thinking

Some tracks or fossils were not intended to be unkind; they were just misguided. Someone gave you an incorrect message or a bad direction. This person may have thought they had your best interest in mind, but either they actually didn't, or they didn't know how their actions would affect you. Change your thinking about others' motives if:

- *They projected their mission onto your life.*
  They may have tried to pass on what they always wanted to be or do rather than what was best for you.
- *They used you for their own selfish rewards.*
  They may have thought they would receive glory from your accomplishments.
- *They tried to pass on their fears.*
  Their experiences with failure caused them to fear, and they tried to pass this on to you. They may even have done it in a caring way, but you do not have to make it part of your life.

Remind Yourself

Remind yourself about the positive imprints. Find and repeat the positive things that people spoke or modeled to you. Also, remember awards you received, successes you achieved,

and the times you were truly aware of the positive influences
in your life.

- Remember awards when you succeeded at doing an outstanding job.
- Accept affirmations when people spoke positive words into your life.
- Gain awareness of the times you really did enjoy something or found you were good at it.

PERSONAL EXERCISE 3.1

Look again at each of the good and bad imprints from Group Exercise B. Let go of others' past sins against you by forgiving. Change what may have been a negative statement or action by rewriting it in a positive way. Remind yourself about the good influences and positive feelings from your past.

THOUGHT 4

You Are Set Up for Success

INNATE TALENTS AND MOTIVATION

In Thought 2, we looked at your current identity. We talked about the values and goals that shape your journey and how you can be guided by the Holy Spirit. In Thought 3, we discussed the influences of the past. Now you have more knowledge for your journey. To get greater clarity on your destiny, though, you need to find the right tools—your talents.

Remember, we often don't see ourselves very well. This doesn't mean our mirror is broken. We simply struggle to understand who we really are. You probably experienced this in earlier in the book if you struggled with some of the questions about your identity. The identity crisis of the Church also affects our self-understanding.

Here is an example: Ask anyone about the famous basketball player Michael Jordan. They will probably tell you what he has done. They may know his scoring records and championship statistics and that he has coached and owned a National Basketball Association team. These are all impressive facts, but they say very little about who Michael Jordan *is*. To learn about his identity, we would need to know about his background and his relationships. For example, Michael is the son of James and Delores Jordan. He was married twice and has five children.

We often focus on what people do before we discover who they really are. These are two completely different things. At any time, the things you do can change. But who you are stays with you your entire life. This chapter will help you focus on who you are. What are your talents—your innate character abilities?

Because we do not see ourselves clearly, it's helpful to use external, objective assessments to discover our tendencies, character, and potential. You can then use the results of these tests to help you take action.

Good tests are objective. This means the results are difficult to manipulate or alter. The insights you receive from the tests should be relatively accurate. Of course, the results do depend on the answers you give. They act as mirrors, reflecting the information you put into them. If you are honest with your answers, you should get an accurate reflection. If you are not truthful, you will get inaccurate results. Either way, the test will act as a mirror.

Let's begin with some definitions.

- *Talent*: A naturally recurring pattern of thought, feeling, or behavior that we can apply productively (put to good use). A talent is a potential strength.
- *Knowledge*: What you know or are aware of. This may be pure facts gained through education. It is also how you make sense of what you know—your understanding. You may gain this by experience.
- *Skills*: The ability to perform the basic steps of an activity. Skills deal with how to do a task. Once you have gained the skill for something, you know how to do it.
- *Strength*: The ability to perform an activity consistently and nearly perfectly. To build your strengths, you identify your talents and add knowledge and skills.

Remember Michael Jordan? He clearly had a talent for playing basketball and became what many consider to be the most perfect basketball player ever to play. He studied the game, listened to his coaches, and practiced constantly. He used knowledge and skills to create a strength.

The tool we will use to assess your talents is called the CliftonStrengths assessment. We are amazed at how accurately this assessment describes our behaviors and motivations. There are other strength and motivational assessments, such as the Myers-Briggs and DiSC assessments. They are good tools, but we don't think they offer the same insight and clarity that the CliftonStrengths assessment does.

BEGINNINGS ARE IMPORTANT

To understand how something works, it helps to know how it began and developed. Here is some information about the CliftonStrengths movement (formerly known as the StrengthsFinder movement) and why it is a useful tool for your personal discovery.

In the early 1950s, the Nebraska School Study Council, with help from the University of Nebraska, conducted a study on ways to improve reading speed and retention. They wanted to know which methods of training worked best. Testing 6,000 tenth-grade students over several years, the study found that the various teaching methods made little difference in reading speeds. However, the study did produce some startling results.

Researchers expected slower-reading students to improve with training more so than the other students. They hypothesized that there was more room for the slower readers to improve and that the better readers would probably be less incentivized to try. Instead, however, researchers found that after training, the students who started out reading the fastest increased their ability even more than those who started out reading slower—*much more.*

Most students initially read at a slower pace of about 90 words per minute. After training, their average speed increased to 150 words per minute. This 67% increase was certainly a good result for any high school student.

Another group of students began reading at an average of 300 words per minute, and after the same training, they increased to an average of

2,900 words per minute! That is an increase of 867%! This amazing result created huge interest and debate throughout the academic world. It became the topic of numerous articles in the areas of education and psychology.

What became clear through this study is not only that there was a difference in the innate abilities of the two groups of students, but there was also a different natural "ceiling" or capability in those students. The group that read at 2,900 words after training clearly had a special talent that could be developed into a strength. Even with the same training, the slower group could not achieve this same strength.

It also seemed clear that the teachers and administrators who thought the faster readers would not improve as much as the slower readers were wrong. The faster students probably did not even know they had such a potential strength. No one would have thought to start training those students to read faster because they were already at a relatively high level.

Based on these results, the Gallup Organization developed a survey tool to identify talents, with the idea that this information would be useful to develop strengths in people and organizations. Donald O. Clifton, a graduate student at the University of Nebraska at the time of the Nebraska School Council Study, was a primary researcher on the project. He eventually became Chairman of Gallup and published the book, *Now, Discover Your Strengths*, in 2001. Gallup is known mostly for its polling but also has a large research and education division.

The first survey Gallup developed and used for this research consisted of 2,000 questions and was given initially to some of the top performers in business, the arts, and many other fields. Over three decades, Gallup interviewed over two million people across 30 different cultures. Gallup identified over 400 talents, which were then grouped into 34 themes. Today, these themes are examined in the CliftonStrengths assessment, a test consisting of 180 questions.

The CliftonStrengths assessment is designed to help people find their talents and develop them into strengths. The assessment reveals a person's main talents, starting with the strongest and moving toward the weakest. Thirty-four is a large number, though. Gallup identified the top five as the best indicators and encourages participants to focus on gaining the most value from those five.

This tool for assessing talents and developing strengths has gained wide acceptance. It is used at major corporations, such as Toyota and Best Buy. A version for educational use, called CliftonStrengths for Students, is used at many major universities.[1]

WHAT ABOUT WEAKNESSES?

People have long focused on improving their weaknesses. It seems logical to do so, but the Gallup results and much research and practical experience over 40 years have shown that concentrating on weaknesses is actually not efficient. It is certainly possible to improve one of your lesser talents. Perhaps you could move talent #34 up to talent #27. But why would you use your time for that instead of focusing on where you are strongest?

In a group, it can be important to manage weaknesses so that the whole group can function together effectively. Another way to say this is focusing on weakness can help prevent failure, but building strengths leads to success.

YOU ARE UNIQUE

Each person has tremendous potential to achieve great things in life. We have talents that can be built into strengths that would enable us to contribute at the pace of a 2,900-word reader, but we do not know what those talents are. The point of this exercise is that in order to reach your goals and move

---

1. This description of the history of strengths-based psychology is an adaptation from the research revealed in *Now, Discover Your Strengths* by The Gallup Organization. Additional information can be found at www.gallupstrengthscenter.com.

toward your destiny, you must learn your talents and develop them into strengths.

This process can be difficult because we often focus on the things we do—the *what* of our lives—rather than *who* we are. When we learn and apply *who* we are first, our lives are more balanced, and our actions are more aligned with our destiny.

How unique are you? In terms of talents, consider this: How many people would you have to ask to find one person with the same top five talents as you, in the same sequence? The answer is about 33 million. Since the world population is around 7.5 billion, there could be about 227 people on earth with the same top five talents in the same sequence.

If you looked for a person with the same top six talents in the same sequence, it would be statistically impossible to find one. The odds of finding one person with the same top eight talents are over one in 700 billion. Remember, too, that this is only a part of what you are. Talents are only one factor of your character. There is no one else exactly like you.

This understanding has an important implication. Because you have a unique identity, nobody can do exactly what you can do. God has created you with specific abilities for specific purposes. This means you are accountable for how you use these abilities.

One way the devil succeeds is by blinding us to our potential. If he can keep you from knowing your giftings and seeing your destiny, you will become a weak, part-time soldier instead of the powerful, full-time warrior God desires. When the Church as a whole recognizes her role and her giftings, the devil will be facing a massive army of warriors battling against him. That will bring tremendous blessing on your community and the entire world, even though the enemy will not like it.

Another reason for understanding and using your talents is that it feels good. As a Christian, there will be an overwhelming joy in your life when your actions align with the talents, gifts, and life mission God has prepared for you.

STRENGTHS (AND WEAKNESSES) IN THE BODY

The psalmist makes it clear that even before we were born, God designed us with a purpose in mind and gave us the abilities to achieve that purpose:

> I praise you because I am fearfully and wonderfully made;
>> your works are wonderful,
>> I know that full well.
>
> My frame was not hidden from you
>> when I was made in the secret place,
>> when I was woven together in the depths of the earth.
>
> Your eyes saw my unformed body;
>> all the days ordained for me were written in your book
>> before one of them came to be (Psalm 139:14–16).

In Thought 2, we learned that all we do as Christians, we do as part of the body of Christ—the Church. We just discussed that we are unique and accountable to use our talents for God. Consequently, we need to look at our talents not only for what they can do for our personal life missions but also for the greater mission of the Church.

As Christians, we are taught to be discerning people—to try to see things clearly. We need to be aware that talents show up and can be used differently in different areas of our lives. For example, if you have the CliftonStrengths talent of **Command**, it might be appropriate for you to take a very strong approach to leadership at your job. Within the Church, however, there might be different lines of authority that require you to use a different approach. You might need to use yet a third approach within your family. This also means that when used in excess or in an inappropriate way, strengths can become weaknesses within a group. Consider this as you function in your strengths.

It is important both to develop talents into strengths and also to learn through experience when and how to use those strengths.

You should also learn the talents and strengths (and weaknesses) of your friends, family, co-workers, and fellow believers in Christ. Take those traits into account when you interact with them. Understanding those traits can assist you in properly assigning tasks in a group and help people function more effectively as a team.

Weakness also has a somewhat unique place in God's culture. Consider Paul's words:

> But he said to me, "My grace is sufficient for you, for my power is made perfect in weakness." Therefore I will boast all the more gladly about my weaknesses, so that Christ's power may rest on me (2 Corinthians 12:9).

The point is not that Paul is "happy" about his weakness. Rather, his trust in the power of Christ allows him to accept the situation he is given. The weakness itself does not help achieve a particular goal, but it magnifies God's strengths. God supplies what is lacking.

God intentionally equipped us with the tools we need for our lives. Paul says, "We are God's handiwork, created in Christ Jesus to do good works, which God prepared in advance for us to do" (Ephesians 2:10). God has plans for the talents He gave you, and He intends to see you make a great contribution with them. It's your job to find out what your talents are and to align yourself with Him.

Imagine this scenario:

> Every day, I walk to work with a bag of tools. And every day, I sit down at my desk and put my bag down. I take out a skill saw and place it on the table. I like having the window open, but the wind makes my papers fly all over the table. It's really frustrating, so I use the saw to hold the papers down. It is a good paper-weight, although it's not good for much else.
>
> I often need to draw a line, so I look for a ruler. The only tool I can find with a straight edge is a file. I try to draw my lines with it, but because of the file's edges, the lines always look zigzag.

I also have to write, so I get my pencil out of the bag. It's a big carpenter's pencil, though, and it's really difficult to write numbers with. I'm always carving a point on it. If I don't pay attention while I'm carving, I can lose focus and carve too much from my pencil. (I love the feeling of woodcarving.) I need to have a really fine point to write numbers because I am an accountant.

Every day, I feel disconnected, as if nothing is working for me. Every day, I take my tools and put them back in my bag. I go home, and the next day I do it all over again. I have had this bag of tools all my life. It should be a major influencing factor in how I approach life.

Imagine how frustrating that life would be. There would be no satisfaction and no reward from using those tools—those talents—because they do not fit the job.

Now it is time for you to look in your tool bag to find out what equipment God has given you. Your tools will be clues to what He wants you to contribute to the world. You'll have more focus when you've aligned yourself with the abilities God has put within you.

To take the CliftonStrengths assessment, follow the instructions in the introduction of this book. You will have 20 seconds to answer each question. To get accurate feedback, please be as honest as possible. There are no right or wrong answers. You will receive your results and a summary explanation immediately after completing the assessment. For a detailed description of each strength, we recommend reading *StrengthsFinder 2.0*. It will be a joy for you to find out how powerfully and wonderfully you are made!

PERSONAL EXERCISE 4.1

How Special Are You?
- When you function in your innate (God-given) talents, which then become strengths, you are naturally more successful at a task than someone without the same talents.

- One in 33 million people have the same five talents in the same order.
- One in 23 billion people have the same six talents in the same order
- One in 700 billion people have the same eight talents in the same order.

"I praise you because I am fearfully and wonderfully made" (Psalm 139:14).

1. List your top five talents (as revealed by CliftonStrengths, DiSC, Myers-Briggs, or other similar assessment).

   a. _____

   b. _____

   c. _____

   d. _____

   e. _____

2. What can you do to add skill or knowledge to your top five talents to make them strengths?

   a. _____

   b. _____

   c. _____

   d. _____

   e. _____

GROUP EXERCISE C

Answer these questions and share your responses with a partner.

1. What negative things have been said to you because others didn't understand your talents or strengths?

_____

_____

_____

2. When have you used your talents or strengths? How did it feel?

_____

_____

_____

Using your dominant hand, write your name five times on the lines below. This is your natural "talent."

_____

_____

_____

_____

Now, use your non-dominant hand to write your name five times. Describe the difference you feel using this hand.

_____

_____

_____

_____

THOUGHT 5

Gifting and Passion

SPIRITUAL GIFTS

These are the spiritual gifts listed in the Bible:

Action	Freedom	Love	Relationships
Beauty	Fulfillment	Meaning	Respect
Comfort	Giving	Mercy	Righteousness
Compassion	Greatness	Nobility	Salvation
Confidence	Harmony	Order	Self-Esteem
Courage	Healing	Organization	Service
Deliverance	Honesty	Passion	Strength
Destiny	Honor	Perseverance	Sympathy
Dignity	Hope	Personal Responsibility	True Success
Discipline	Inner Peace	Positive Attitude	Truth
Dreams	Inspiration	Possibilities	Value
Endurance	Integrity	Potential	Victory
Excellence	Intimacy	Prosperity	Wholeness
Excitement	Joy	Protection	Worship
Faith	Justice	Purpose	
Faithfulness	Life	Reality	

God has placed a gift in every person. He leaves no one out. As you read the following verses, ask yourself what your special gift is.

For by the grace given me I say to every one of you: Do not think of yourself more highly than you ought, but rather think of yourself with sober judgment, in accordance with the faith God has distributed to each of you. For just as each of us has one body with many members, and these members do not all have the same function, so in Christ we, though many, form one body, and each member belongs to all the others. We have different gifts, according to the grace given to each of us. If your gift is prophesying, then prophesy in accordance with your faith; if it is serving, then serve; if it is teaching, then teach; if it is to encourage, then give encouragement; if it is giving, then give generously; if it is to lead, do it diligently; if it is to show mercy, do it cheerfully (Romans 12:3–8).

Paul instructs believers to think of themselves "with sober judgment"—with humility instead of pride. As we learn to recognize our gifts, we must continue to stay humble. It is tempting to take the credit when we succeed at something, but remember: our gifts come from God, not our own efforts or abilities. God intentionally gives specific gifts to each person, so we should stand in humility and confidence.

No particular gift is more important than another. They simply have different functions (Romans 12:4). Imagine a ruler with each gift occupying half an inch of space. Is the space that comes just after "6" better than the space just before "8"? No, of course not. They're merely different. What is important is that each space increases the length of the ruler. Similarly, the more people use their gifts, the more others are helped. To use another illustration, gifts are like tools, and the body of Christ is the tool belt. When a tool belt has more tools, the carpenter (God) can build, repair, and restore more than ever before.

God deposited a gift of His choosing inside each one of us. He gave it to us for a purpose—to do something with it. See if you can find the purpose of your gift in this passage:

Each of you should use whatever gift you have received to serve others, as faithful stewards of God's grace in its various forms. If anyone speaks, they should do so as one who speaks the very words of God. If anyone serves, they should do so with the strength God provides, so that in all things God may be praised through Jesus Christ. To him be the glory and the power for ever and ever. Amen (1 Peter 4:10–11).

Did you see the purpose? Our gifts are meant to serve others. They aren't for us or about us; they are not meant to promote us or glorify us. They are to give away and help others.

Through the Holy Spirit, God provides gifts to empower and motivate us. Peter says we should always direct people back to the gifts' source—God. We must give Him the proper credit. When you receive a package from a delivery service, you may thank the delivery person, but you really recognize and thank the person who sent the gift. As Christians, we simply deliver the gifts God has given to us for others.

When we use our gifts, we bless those both inside and outside the Church:

Outside the Church

"In the same way, let your light shine before others, that they may see your good deeds and glorify your Father in heaven" (Matthew 5:16).

Inside the Church

From whom the whole body, joined and knit together by what every joint supplies, according to the effective working by which every part does its share, causes growth of the body for the edifying of itself in love
(Ephesians 4:16 NKJV).

PERSONAL EXERCISE 5.1

We all serve people in different ways. Complete the following exercise to find how you best serve others.

Take the Spiritual Gifts assessment found at
http://gatewaypeople.com/ministries/id/events/id-seminar

1. List your top three Spiritual Gifts from the test.

   a. _____

   b. _____

   c. _____

2. How can you use each gift to serve others?

   a. _____

   b. _____

   c. _____

TAKING ACTION ON YOUR GIFTS

Action Words to Consider

Achieve	Create	Extend	Mold	Restore
Acquire	Decide	Facilitate	Motivate	Return
Adopt	Defend	Finance	Move	Revise
Advance	Delight	Forgive	Negotiate	Sacrifice
Affect	Demonstrate	Foster	Nurture	Safeguard
Alleviate	Develop	Franchise	Obtain	Satisfy
Appreciate	Devise	Further	Open	Save
Ascend	Direct	Gather	Organize	Sell
Authenticate	Discover	Generate	Participate	Serve

Believe	Discuss	Give	Persuade	Share
Brighten	Distribute	Hold	Practice	Speak
Build	Draft	Host	Prepare	Stand
Call	Dream	Identify	Present	Summon
Cause	Drive	Ignite	Produce	Support
Choose	Ease	Illuminate	Progress	Surrender
Claim	Educate	Implement	Promise	Sustain
Collect	Elect	Improve	Promote	Take
Command	Embrace	Improvise	Provide	Tap
Communicate	Encourage	Inspire	Realize	Touch
Compete	Endow	Integrate	Receive	Trade
Complete	Engage	Intensify	Reclaim	Translate
Compliment	Engineer	Involve	Refine	Understand
Compose	Enhance	Keep	Reflect	Unite
Conceive	Enlighten	Know	Regard	Uphold
Confirm	Enlist	Labor	Relate	Use
Connect	Entertain	Launch	Relax	Value
Consider	Enthuse	Lead	Release	Verbalize
Construct	Envision	Master	Rely	Verify
Contact	Evaluate	Mature	Remember	Volunteer
Continue	Excite	Measure	Renew	Work
Convey	Explore	Mediate	Resonate	Write
Counsel	Express	Model	Respect	

PERSONAL EXERCISE 5.2

Your gifts are for serving or doing something for others. "Doing" is an action. Look at the list of action words and circle the words that seem particularly important or inspiring to you. Next, narrow your list to the six words that most excite you and write them on the lines below.

1. _____

2. _____

3. _____

4. _____

5. _____

6. _____

Review these six action words and make sure they inspire and excite you. If they don't, recheck your circled words and find your top six action words.

Next, choose the three most important words in order of priority or how much they inspire you. It may help to ask, "If I could only do one of these six things, which would it be?"

List your top three action words and top three talents/strengths. Then draw a line from each action word to the talent/strength it matches most closely. Do these actions words express your talents/strengths in action?

Top 3 Action Words	Top 3 Talents/Strengths
1. _____	1. _____
2. _____	2. _____
3. _____	3. _____

Now list your top three action words and top three spiritual gifts. Draw a line from each action word to the spiritual gift it matches most closely. Do these action words express your spiritual gifts in action?

Top 3 Action Words	Top 3 Spiritual Gifts
1. _____	1. _____
2. _____	2. _____
3. _____	3. _____

GROUP EXERCISE D

Complete the following exercises with a partner.

1. Explain why your action words excite you.
2. Explain why you placed them in the order you did.
3. Explain how your action words describe your talents/strengths and gifts.
4. Finish this statement: "I want to (action word 1), (action word 2), and (action word 3)." How does this statement make you feel?

PASSION OR HOLY DISCONTENT

Awake, my soul, stretch every nerve,
And press with vigor on;
A heav'nly race demands thy zeal,
And an immortal crown.

—Philip Doddridge

What is your purpose? What excites you? What do you do so well and receive so much joy doing that you would do it without pay? What is your *passion*?

After talents/strengths and spiritual gifts comes the third element of what God has given you to achieve His purpose for your life. Bill Hybels examines this final piece in his book, *Holy Discontent*. In it, he describes how each of us has an issue, idea, or involvement around which we can eagerly say, "Something has to be done to change this, and I will just burst if it has to go on like this for much longer."

Call it *holy discontent*. Call it a *passion*. Whatever you call it, it is real, it is important, and it gets you excited. The problem is that many of us have lost our ability to connect with this passion. It has been replaced by what author Charles Hummel calls the "tyranny of the urgent." Too many issues seem urgent and demand our focus and time; they distract us from connecting with what is important and really excites us.

Do you know your passion? Can you describe it? Can you see it in the world around you? It usually looks like a need or something that's broken and could be so much better. It may be about the environment, politics, legal matters, or Christian beliefs. It may be about international missions, the parent-teacher organization at your child's school, or care for the elderly.

Whatever it is, God has given you a special dissatisfaction with the status quo in that particular area. He has given you a powerful desire to change the situation. Even if you cannot see it right now, the holy discontent is there.

Think about what bothers you most in the world. Look at the news, go to a movie, or observe society around you with the eyes of an investigator. Ask God to reveal what He has wired you to be passionate about. If you feel your heart pounding about an issue, take notice! You may have found your passion.

Another way to identify your passion is to find areas in which you have excelled. Working in our areas of passion provides deep satisfaction and increased energy. We can discover a passion area without even realizing it; for some unexplained reason, it seems to come naturally, and we become very good at tasks related to that passion. It's like placing a sailboat in the ocean. The currents and wind will naturally carry the boat in some direction. Where has the current of your passion carried you? Can you see the direction in which you have floated?

Of course, as someone has said, "Hope is not a plan." We don't want to leave the direction of our life in the hands of hope—hope that life's current will carry us to the correct island of our life mission. When you travel by boat, you do not allow the wind, waves, and current to decide where you go. Instead, you chart a course to the location of your choosing and then sail to it.

Many people allow the current of life to push and pull them because they don't know why they're on the planet. They say, "I hope it all works out," or "I guess we'll just have to see what happens." When you learn your passion, though, you find a clear purpose. Can you imagine waking up in the morning, taking a deep breath, and knowing precisely why you're here? Your day could be filled with excitement and a deep sense of purpose.

Three Kinds of Passion

> *Life is too short to be little.*
> *Man is never so manly as when he feels deeply,*
> *acts boldly, and expresses himself with*
> *frankness and with fervor.*
>
> —Benjamin Disraeli

There are various kinds of passion, but we want to focus on these three: personal passion, general passion, and genuine passion.

Personal Passion

Brad: In my early adult life, I read books and attended seminars to help develop life goals and mission statements. They often asked a question like, "What would you do if you could do anything, knew you wouldn't fail, and money wasn't an object?" Finally—a question I could quickly and easily answer!

I would spend my life on a sailboat in the Bahamas—casually sailing around the islands, stopping to scuba dive, and going to port long enough to buy supplies. What could be better than that?

We can easily identify personal passions because they are all about what we want, need, or deserve.

Personal passion makes us think, "Wouldn't the world be a much better place if everyone lived the way I think they should?" Personal passion usually places us at the center of the universe, where we believe everything should peacefully revolve around our wishes.

I am glad I took my "sailing in the Bahamas" answer one step further. I asked myself, "Would I really want to do this forever? Would anyone benefit from this besides me?" As I projected living out my new nautical life mission for a week, a month, a year … I quickly realized that personal passions are fun and self-satisfying, but they are usually shallow and unfulfilling if we make them our life's pursuit.

Personal passions are not necessarily wrong, but we need to make sure we put them in the right priority. They make wonderful hobbies or recreational activities that refresh us during difficult times. We must realize, however, that there is more to our existence than dedicating our lives to self-absorbed activities that only benefit us.

General Passion

General passion, on the other hand, is about helping others. When watching the news, you may see a story about the plight of a person or group that moves you deeply. You think, "Somebody should do something about this." But then you change the channel, watch a movie, and make a snack. That news story stirred an emotional response in your mind, but it didn't reach the depths of your heart.

The world is filled with wonderful opportunities to do great things, but every story or cause stirs our emotions in different ways. Perhaps a friend has told you with great emotion about a cause he was working on, and you simply said, "That's nice." It's likely your friend didn't understand your reply because he expected a much stronger, more passionate response. You did agree that it was a good cause, but it did not move you the way it moved your friend.

Your friend's passion that brought out such great emotion in him was only a general passion to you. It is good, and somebody should do something about it, but it did not move you to action. People are passionate about different things, and that's the way it should be. Don't feel guilty for not experiencing passion about a cause as deeply as someone else.

Genuine Passion

Genuine passion makes a person say, "I *must* do something about this." It's the thing over which you would feel deep regret not making a significant difference before you died.

Concerning genuine passion, there are two primary groups of people. The first group is filled with those whose passion is built into them. Like unanchored boats, they are moved by an invisible force in some general direction. Certain fields of study, reading material, hobbies, friends, and role models mysteriously attract them. Some people in this group can't even describe their passion well. They don't recognize the common thread of interest that runs through their life. Others in this group have identified their strong feelings about a cause but can't explain why they're so passionate about it; they simply know that it truly interests them.

The second group has suffered some deep emotional pain, and they want to protect others from the same experience. Some people had difficult teenage years, and they now have a passion to help teenagers work through hard decisions and situations. One woman spent her childhood moving from state to state because of her father's job. As an adult, she married a man whose job led to even more relocations. She now has a sense of purpose and calling to help others feel welcome in new surroundings, especially the women who move into her community.

This group is best explained by Paul's words:

> He [God] comes alongside us when we go through hard times, and before you know it, he brings us alongside someone else who is going through hard times so that we can be there for that person just as God was there for us (2 Corinthians 1:4 MSG).

No matter which group you're in, it's important to identify your passion and learn to describe it. You will be the most passionate person for what interests and excites you.

PERSONAL EXERCISE 5.3

1. Genuine Passion: I must make a difference.
2. General Passion: Somebody should do something.
3. Personal Passion: This is a hobby.

In the space to the right of the triangle, list some things that fall in area #2 General Passion and area #3 Personal Passion. You will fill in area #1 later.

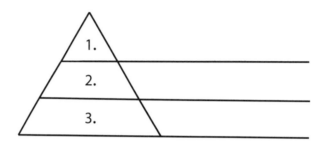

SIGNS OF PASSION

How do you know you have genuine passion?

Urgency

- What tasks seem to jump to the top of your to-do list?
- What problem could get your assistance at 2:00 a.m.?

Endurance

- What projects have you been able to work on without becoming tired?
- What needs are you willing to help meet even when you are exhausted?

Excitement

- What causes or "people-needs" excite you?
- What conversations make you to feel alive?

The following exercise is designed to help you identify and describe your genuine passion. Take your time to work through the questions and answer them carefully. Some of the questions are followed by another question: "Why?" This will allow you to think more about your response and why you answered the way you did.

PERSONAL EXERCISE 5.4

1. When watching the news, what kind of story makes you feel the strongest emotions? Why?

_____

_____

_____

2. What topics do you love to talk about for long periods of time? Why?

_____

_____

_____

3. What tasks or projects seem to create endless energy for you? What do you enjoy most about them? Why?

_____

_____

_____

4. What problem or pain do other people experience that you feel passionate about and wish you could eliminate? Why do you feel so strongly about this issue?

_____

_____

_____

5. If you could completely eliminate just one problem, pain, or sin in the world, what would it be? Why?

_____

_____

_____

6. What job would you do for free if money were not an issue? Why?

_____

_____

_____

7. Is there a recognizable theme among your answers? What is it?

_____

_____

_____

8. Look for the common element among your previous answers. Is there:
   a. A pain or problem to be eliminated? Describe it in one word:

_____

_____

   b. A cause or group of people to help? Describe it in one word:

_____

_____

   c. What is the end result, cure, or solution you would like to see? Describe it in one word:

_____

_____

_____

PERSONAL EXERCISE 5.5

My Genuine Passion

"It is fine to be zealous, provided the purpose is good, and to be so always, not just when I am with you" (Galatians 4:18).

Your passion should lead to actions that leave matters better than they were before. Does your answer to Personal Exercise 5.4, question #8c match any of the words on this list? If so, circle it. Do you like a word on this list better than the one in your answer? If so, change your answer.

Action	Freedom	Love	Relationships
Beauty	Fulfillment	Meaning	Respect
Comfort	Giving	Mercy	Righteousness
Compassion	Greatness	Nobility	Salvation
Confidence	Harmony	Order	Self-Esteem
Courage	Healing	Organization	Service
Deliverance	Honesty	Passion	Strength
Destiny	Honor	Perseverance	Sympathy
Dignity	Hope	Personal Responsibility	True Success
Discipline	Inner Peace	Positive Attitude	Truth
Dreams	Inspiration	Possibilities	Value
Endurance	Integrity	Potential	Victory
Excellence	Intimacy	Prosperity	Wholeness
Excitement	Joy	Protection	Worship
Faith	Justice	Purpose	
Faithfulness	Life	Reality	

Use your answers from Personal Exercise 5.4 to create your genuine passion.

My passion is to (give, provide, show, etc.) _____

(choose one from #8c)

(to the, for, etc.)_____

(choose one from #8a or #8b)

Try saying it in different ways. Which do you like the best?

Write your answer in area #1 of the triangle in Personal Exercise 5.3. Share your response with a partner and explain why this passion is so important to you. Don't get frustrated if they don't feel the same intense emotional connection to this passion that you do. This is *your* genuine passion. Your partner may see it as a general passion and be glad that you're excited about it.

PERSONAL EXERCISE 5.6

Summarize Your Findings

Top 3 Action Words from Personal Exercise 5.2

1. _____

2. _____

3. _____

Top 3 Talents/Strengths from Personal Exercise 5.2

1. _____

2. _____

3. _____

Top 3 Spiritual Gifts from Personal Exercise 5.2

1. _____

2. _____

3. _____

1. Genuine Passion from Personal Exercise 5.3: I must make a difference.

    _____

2. General Passion from Personal Exercise 5.3: Somebody should do
    something.

    _____

3. Personal Passion from Personal Exercise 5.3: This is a hobby.

    _____

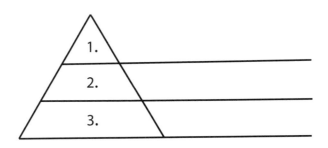

1. What is the pain or problem to be eliminated?
    (Personal Exercise 5.4, #8a).

    _____

    _____

2. What is the cause or group of people to help?
    (Personal Exercise 5.4, #8b).

    _____

    _____

3. What is the end result, cure, or solution you would like to see
    reached? (Personal Exercise 5.4, #8c.)

    _____

    _____

Look over these results and make sure they sound right to you. Does the information excite or stir you? Explain.

_____

_____

_____

_____

_____

_____

_____

_____

_____

_____

_____

THOUGHT 6

Honest Reflections

JUST A GLIMPSE

God's plan for your life mission can become clearer when you examine the places where your passion, talents, and spiritual gifts overlap or connect. Obviously, there can be many clues to your destiny, but these three tend to be the most difficult to discern. They also represent the majority of the drive behind your deep inner hunger. Other factors like experiences, time, and resources do point to your calling, but not with the same level of power.

Look at the diagram below and insert the contributing pieces you have identified up to this point.

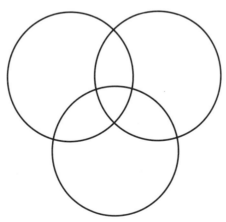

The place where these three factors (passion, talents, and spiritual gifts) meet will help you see God's intent for you. It is not the whole picture, but you can glimpse the outline. After you examine and define these three concepts, you should begin to see God's life mission for you.

Malcolm Gladwell explains the value of this "first glimpse" in his book *Blink: The Power of Thinking without Thinking*. He talks about a concept he calls "thin-slicing" and shows how just a small cross-section of something—a "thin slice"—can reveal a great deal about the whole item.

Allan: I have an example of this concept from my years of competitive swimming:

One of my trainers suggested I get a muscle biopsy to determine the kinds of swimming races I should enter. I went to a sports medicine doctor who specialized in this procedure and knew how to interpret the results. I was not prepared for what happened. The doctor plunged a huge needle deep into a large muscle. He then withdrew the needle, which now contained some of my muscle tissue. When he examined the tissue, he could tell whether most of the muscle fibers were fast-twitch or slow-twitch. This would determine whether I should enter long, slow races or short, fast races. A high percentage of fast-twitch muscle fibers indicates an athlete will do better in short races. A high percentage of slow-twitch muscle fibers points to long races.

The procedure was quite painful, but it did help me figure out which kinds of races my body was built to swim. I had more fast-twitch muscle fibers, so I was made to be a "sprinter."

This discovery was good news because I had always had difficulty training for distance swimming. My coach had even thought that I must be lazy. I was relieved to discover I was made for sprinting. When I focused on sprinting—my innate ability—I progressed rapidly because I was made for it.

I owe my focus, redirection, and success as a swimmer to the knowledge that came from a thin slice of my muscle.

You can use a "thin slice" of your three primary factors to get a picture of your identity and then build on it. A brief look at these three factors will show you how they contribute to the end result.

Passion

Passion provides energy and motivation to act on our life mission. It is crucial in our lives because it comes from the heart. Jesus said, "Out of the abundance of the heart the mouth speaks" (Matthew 12:34 NKJV).

God is most concerned with our hearts. When our hearts are engaged with an idea from Him, we feel His energy and focus. This kind of passion is aimed at issues or people-groups that need development or help.

Physical and Character Talents

Both physical and character talents naturally equip us to do things well. God gave us these abilities, and once we see how they overlap with our passions, it becomes clear that He planted them in us for a purpose from the very beginning.

Allan: My physical talent to swim enabled me to receive a scholarship to the University of Nebraska, where I met my wife. Our marriage enabled me to live in the United States rather than South Africa. My ability to swim competitively and living in the United States opened up a new set of opportunities I never could have imagined.

What physical or other ability do you have that could turn into a special path of destiny?

You also have character talents, such as those revealed through the CliftonStrengths assessment. When you build your talents into strengths, they can enable you to make world-class contributions. Character talents can be harder to identify, so a "mirror" assessment is helpful. You must also use skills and knowledge to develop your talents into consistent strengths. This effort is rewarded as we discover the activities that bring us joy and suit our aptitude. We find what we were made to do!

Spiritual Gifts

Spiritual gifts are the other abilities God gives us. These abilities may correspond with our talents, enhancing them like a special infusion, or they may enable us to accomplish different things.

God's spiritual gifts equip every believer to perform acts of service in ways we cannot do on our own. When we know our gifts, we can intentionally develop them to become more effective in serving others. It is simply good stewardship to know what you have and with God's help and guidance, do what you can to make it better.

The Intersection of Three Factors

At the intersection of these three critical factors, you should be able to see a thin slice of your life mission. As you think about it, perhaps you can feel your pulse quicken. If it engages your spiritual heart, passion will exist, and when true passion exists, the physical heart speeds up. This is a good indication that you are probably seeing your life mission.

However, you are not finished yet. There is still some work to do in order to test and clarify your mission. Get comfortable with it and be able to communicate it. The next step will be to discuss it with others.

CONSIDER THE INFLUENCE OF FRIENDSHIP

Once you have a glimpse of these three overlapping factors, share it with a friend. First, though, consider carefully what kind of friend you can tell. Not all your friends may be interested in your plans, and this could be for a number of reasons. They may be absorbed in their own lives. They may not have time to spend with you. Some will even feel threatened or jealous. Don't share your thoughts with people such as these.

Instead, find a friend whom you can trust to have your best interests at heart:

- Someone who knows you well and will hold you accountable to what you can become
- Someone who is not afraid to challenge you if you're aiming too low
- Someone who will faithfully support you as you reach higher than either of you may have reached in the past
- Someone whose relationship with you is strong enough to survive a confrontation or disagreement

Tell this friend what you are thinking, what you are seeking, and how important it is to you. Explain the thin slice you have seen of what your life mission might be and ask them for feedback. Don't try to do it all at once. Let them comment on each factor of the mission as well as how they fit together. This input can help inspire you and expand your vision.

As you think about what your friends and family say about your quest, pay close attention to who says what and what role each person plays in your life. In his book *Vital Friends*, Tom Rath discusses the critical role friends play in our achievements. Consider for a moment why you do what you do. Why do you work? Why do you coach? Why do you volunteer? With whom do you go out to eat, watch a sporting event, or pray? Much of what we do is done *with*, *for*, or *because of* a friend or family member. These relationships heavily influence the things we pursue. We're designed by God to live this way—in relationships—which is why you should bring your friends and family into the discussion at this point.

> **Allan:** When I was a teenager, I was an average competitive swimmer with average training habits. One day during practice, my coach pulled me out of my swimming lane and sat me down on the diving board next to the pool. I thought I was in trouble for how I practiced that day.

Instead, my coach began to tell me very seriously that I had the potential to become a world-class athlete—that I could be ranked among the top 25 swimmers in the world. He had seen that ability in me early in my training, but he wanted to know if I would stay in the program.

That day, everything about swimming changed for me. I believed my coach. I became more serious about swimming and started going to practice every day, doing extra when I could. I began going to more swim meets and racing with intention. I believed my coach, and I wanted to see it happen. His larger-than-life challenge stretched me to reach for a goal I had never thought possible.

Today, I have a world swimming record hanging on the wall in my office and numerous gold medals and trophies. I won these in an activity I first began only because my best friend's mom was a swimming teacher. The point of this story is that without the challenge from a friend (my coach), I don't know that I would have risen to that level in swimming. I needed someone else to affirm the ability I already had but not just anyone—I needed someone I trusted and who could speak to me openly and honestly. I'm sure if you think about your past, you'll recall instances in which you made an important decision concerning your future, and somewhere in that decision is the support of a trusted friend or family member.

PERSONAL EXERCISE 6.1

Share your discoveries—your passions, talents/strengths, and spiritual gifts—with a friend or family member this week. Ask this person to hold you accountable and to check up on your progress throughout this process.

Caution

- Make sure this person knows you well and believes in you.
- It's okay to be nervous; you are sharing deep feelings.
- Listen openly. Don't try to influence their feedback in a positive or negative way.
- Write down their feedback so you can refer to it along with your other discoveries.

After you share your answers with your chosen person, evaluate their advice. Friends and family members can be painfully discerning when they are honest and thoughtful. Unfortunately, the same people may be threatened by your new awakening and may try to pull you back. Advice can sharpen and strengthen what God is awakening in you, but it can also steer you away from the light now emerging in your life. Evaluating advice is an important step in balancing the life mission you will embrace.

If you carefully choose a trusted person to share your search for your life mission, then you are more likely to get good advice. Another good way to manage advice is to tell people what you expect. Let your trusted person know what you are doing and why. Tell them how disconnected you've felt and how long you've lived with this hunger—that *more* is available and indeed is expected of you. Tell them you are ready to make big changes in your life, and this represents one of the most important life changes you will ever make. The seriousness of your words will help them respond properly to your thoughts and be more honest with you.

Ask your trusted person to respond to you with words that will encourage you. Ask them to express criticism or negative thoughts in as positive and balanced a way as possible. As you know, it is already easy to avoid our life mission. John 10:10 says the devil wants to steal, kill, and destroy. He wants to prevent you from fully awakening to God's purpose for your life. This will be his chance to discourage and distract you. Be ready— protect your vision and your heart.

When others advise you, look for insights that bring clarity, challenge you, and expand your life mission. Clarity is important because it may contain an element of focus you haven't considered—one that expands the scope of your vision. But advice may also redirect your focus out of your area of interest or passion. In this case, your friend or family member is probably replacing your vision and desire with their own. Remember, there's time to help them develop their vision, but this time is intended for your vision development. Stay on course.

PERSONAL EXERCISE 6.2

Spend the next week examining your discoveries. Question them to make sure they point to your life mission. Ask yourself the following questions as they apply.

1. Would my career change? If so, how?

   _____

   _____

   _____

2. Would my spouse's role have to change?

   _____

   _____

   _____

3. What would a change like this do to my parenting role?

   _____

   _____

   _____

4. How would my relationships change with my family and friends?

   _____

   _____

   _____

THOUGHT 7

Embracing Your Mission and Vision

REMEMBER THE POWER OF WORDS

As you create and refine your vision and mission statements, consider the power of words.

Proverbs 18:21 reminds us, "The tongue has the power of life and death." Words have tremendous creative power. In fact, they're the very channel of all creation. When God created "the heavens and the earth" (Genesis 1:1), He did not use earthmoving equipment. He simply spoke words, and everything came into existence.

All of your words have power. Some will do good and build up; others will do evil and destroy. Jesus says that if we have faith, we can tell a mountain, "Go, throw yourself into the sea," and the mountain will obey! (Matthew 21:21). Think carefully about your vision and mission statements, knowing the words you use will bring into existence that which you speak.

YOUR VISION STATEMENT

Without prophetic vision, people abandon restraint.

—Proverbs 29:18 (ISV)

A vision statement should be a short, one-sentence summary of how you see your destiny. This is where you answer the question of "what" you want to be, *not* "how" you will do it. We will deal with the "how" question later.

Your vision statement should be easy to remember, easy for others to understand, and exciting to you. It should also remain consistent over time. The following exercise will use the information gathered to this point in the book to help you create a simple, powerful vision statement for your life.

PERSONAL EXERCISE 7.1

The diagram on the next page represents two pieces of land separated by a deep valley. Refer to Personal Exercise 5.6 to find your answers to the questions.

On the left side of the valley is the "Who? Cause/Group" line. Above it, write the cause or group of people you're passionate to help. Next, on the right side of the valley is the "End Results?" line. Above it, write what you desire to be the end result, cure, or solution. Finally, at the bottom of the valley is the "What is wrong? Pain/Problem?" line. Above it, write the pain or problem you want to eliminate.

After filling in these three lines, you should be able to complete this statement:

"I want to help (*Cause/Group*) keep from falling off the cliff and being destroyed by (*Pain/Problem*) and reach a place where they can be or find (*End Result*)."

Another way to say it is:

"I exist to provide (**End Result**) for (**Cause/Group**) and stop (**Pain/Problem**).

Does either statement work for you? Sometimes you have to rearrange the wording to help the sentence make sense. The point is to make sure you have a cause or group that is reaching a safe destination and avoiding a problem.

Make sure your statement hits the center of your passion. Don't settle for something close. All three factors should stir you emotionally. If not, you may not have found part of your vision.

Occasionally people find it difficult to choose words for each of the three areas. If you are having similar trouble, you can do this exercise using any one of the three and rework it to bring more clarity. For example, let's say you only know the end result, which you have labeled "hope." You know with great conviction that you must bring hope. Now ask yourself, "Who is currently living without hope?" Which less fortunate cause or group of people moves you the most? For this example, suppose it is "inner city children." One last question: "What is happening to inner city children that concerns you deeply and exhibits hopelessness?" Let's say the pain/problem is "hunger."

Use these answers to complete both statements:
- "I want to help *inner city children* keep from falling off the cliff and being destroyed by *hunger* and reach a place where they can find *hope*."
- "I exist to provide **hope** for **inner city children** and stop **hunger**."

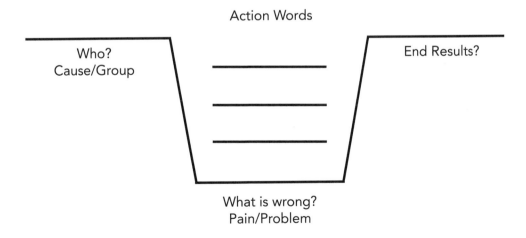

To complete the diagram, return to Personal Exercise 5.6 and find the three action words that express your spiritual gifts and talents/strengths. Write them on the lines below "Action Words." Your action words will be the bridge that carries the Cause/Group safely to the End Result.

PERSONAL EXERCISE 7.2

Write Your Vision Statement.
Here are two ways to write your vision statement. Use the one that best fits your words.

1. I exist to provide, give, offer, or supply:

_____	_____	_____
(end result)	(to/in/for)	(cause/group)

through, by, with:

_____	_____	_____
(action word)	(action word)	(action word)

2. I exist to eliminate, remove, reduce, or eradicate:

_____	_____	_____
(pain/problem)	(to/in/from)	(cause/group)

through, by, with:

_____	_____	_____
(action word)	(action word)	(action word)

GROUP EXERCISE E

Thinking about your vision statement, ask yourself these questions. Then share your responses with a partner.

- Does it excite me? In what ways?
- Does it motivate me toward action? How?
- Does the statement clarify my life mission? How?
- Does it focus my passion? In what way?

MISSION STATEMENT

Most people overestimate what they can do in a day and underestimate what they can do in a lifetime.

—Anonymous

Your mission statement will explain *how* you will accomplish your vision. Here the process shifts from the "what" of your destiny to measurable action items. Be open to many ideas. You may adjust your mission statement over time. As you accomplish portions of it, or as society and technology change, you may need to alter "how" you achieve your vision.

Be aware that two people with passion to help the same cause or group can move in totally different directions. Each of us has different talents/strengths and spiritual gifts that work in unique ways (action words). Responses may be different, and that is okay. The action items of your mission statement will describe how God designed *you* to help.

Thinking about these action items should excite you because they're going to help the cause or group you are passionate about. Your mission statement should challenge the borders of your capabilities because it's bigger than you are. The things you're about to write should describe something that could require the rest of your life to accomplish. This is your life mission—the action items to do for your vision statement.

PERSONAL EXERCISE 7.3

Using your three action words from Personal Exercise 7.1, fill in the blank spaces below. Then ask yourself how you'll act using these words to fulfill your vision.

For example, if your first action word is "teach," your answer could look like this:

I will *teach* by:

- *Teaching classes in my church or community organization*
- *Writing articles or creating videos that teach others*
- *Being an example and modeling the message for my coworkers and community*

Try it. You may want to write in pencil in case you want to make changes later.

1. I will _____ by:
   - _____
   - _____
   - _____

2. I will _____ by:
   - _____
   - _____
   - _____

3. I will _____ by:
   - _____
   - _____
   - _____

Now read each action item and ask yourself these questions:

- Is this action item directed toward helping the cause/group I'm passionate about?
- Will this action item help me reach the end result of my vision?
- Will this action item help fix the pain/problem I identified as important to me?

Any action item that did not lead to a "yes" answer for each question needs to be adjusted. Refine your action items as needed in order to produce your final mission statement. Now that you know who you are, you know the direction of your destiny.

How closely does your actual life reflect your life mission? Look at your daily activities while thinking about your newly defined vision and mission statements. You may find pieces of your mission in the things you're already doing. Maybe some parts of your job allow you to do things consistent with your identity. Do you have activities or projects that just need minor adjustments to help your life mission? Perhaps you're volunteering in a community organization that hits your passion area, but a different role in the organization would make better use of your gifts and talents. Other action items may need major work or redirection.

Brad: I helped someone who, after completing these exercises, realized they were already doing some of their mission. But they had never really defined it, so they did not know if they were succeeding. Like an archer shooting arrows into a fog, they could not tell if they should celebrate for hitting the target or if they needed to adjust their aim for a second shot. Once the fog lifted as they defined their life mission, they could see the target. They could celebrate each time they hit it and make intelligent adjustments when they missed. This clearer vision allowed them to make intentional decisions that helped them align with their life mission. Their identity allowed them to move toward their destiny.

GROUP EXERCISE F

Answer these questions and share your responses with a partner.
- How clearly do you understand your mission?
- How can you adjust your activities to spend more time making progress on your God-ordained mission?
- How has this exercise helped you refocus or redefine your identity?

THOUGHT 8

Can It Really Happen?

The heights charm us, but the steps do not;
with the mountain in our view we love to walk the plains.
—Johann Wolfgang von Goethe

It is time to take action. It is good to have vision and mission statements, but if you don't take steps toward making them a reality, then we will have failed our purpose for this book.

You have become aware of your identity and the potential inside you and set a direction for action. In this final section, we will give you a list of tools to use along your journey. You may not follow these steps in this exact order, but we believe each is important and helpful.

LEARN

Try to learn as much as possible about the cause or group of your mission and the problems facing it/them. You may be aware of the need but do not have enough knowledge to proceed. Start by asking these questions:

- *Who?* (Is anybody already doing this?)
- *How?* (How have they done it?)

- *How much?* (How big is the problem? How great is the need?)
- *What?* (Is there more than one way to address the need?)

REORGANIZE

Chances are your current lifestyle and activities don't fully help you walk in your life mission. You may need to reorganize your activities and address some issues, taking time each day to move toward your mission. These issues can include:

- *Priorities*: What needs to be moved to the front or the back of your list of important tasks or activities?
- *Time*: How much time will you need to work toward your mission? How can you adjust your daily schedule to give you this time?
- *Focus:* How can you focus more attention on your mission?

While we are on this subject, let's address the issue of money. Some people may tell you that if you are pursuing your dreams, you will be able to accomplish anything you want. They may also say that if you find your true calling and work toward it, it will not seem like "work" and will "all work out." They may imply that funding or other resources will not become a problem.

Life does not always work this way, though. If you have enough money to change course and pursue your mission already, you are the exception. For most people, your mission may not be what pays your bills right now. In that case, patiently take whatever steps you can to move in the direction of your mission, knowing that your mission may never provide all your income.

Consider the apostle Paul. Sometimes other believers supported him, and he was able to carry out his mission full time. At other times, he had to work as a tentmaker while still carrying out his mission (see Acts 18:3).

BE RESPONSIBLE

Keep in mind that you should pursue your mission not only because you can make a contribution to your cause and receive personal joy from doing so, but also because you are a steward of God's gifts. He gave you gifts and talents for a reason. Remember the parable of the talents in Matthew 25. God holds us accountable for the ways we use our talents. He does not seem to be concerned about the amount of return we generate but rather that each of His laborers (disciples) takes some sort of action to invest their talents. God will grow and harvest the fruit from the seeds of effort we plant. We are responsible to know what our gifts and talents are and to make sure we use them.

> I planted the seed, Apollos watered it, but God has been making it grow
> (1 Corinthians 3:6).

God's Timing

Throughout this course we have discussed a number of practical things to help you move toward the life mission God has shown you. Pray about these things and ask for His direction. Do this continually as you work toward your mission. For each step, try to identify if God is directing you to move or to wait. Sometimes we need to move forward boldly with an action. Other times we need to wait, evaluate the results of our actions, and listen for God to tell us what we should do next.

Tracks and Fossils

Can you identify anything from your past—tracks or fossils—that might be hindering your progress? Be aware that you may find new tracks along the way.

People Who Can Help

Few great accomplishments are ever achieved alone. Even Mother Teresa had mentors and supporters during her long time of service. Identify what kinds of people you need for support. Are they people you know? Who else could you look for? How would you contact them?

DIRECTION

Direction is tied to reorganization. You may have heard, "A journey starts with a single step," but there are many more steps to follow.

Look at your action items and make them into a list of steps to take. What must you do first? If you are not good at this kind of planning, find someone who is and ask them to help you create a step-by-step plan. See what steps can be taken today and commit to doing something every day to live your dream, even if it is something small.

Some steps may seem too big to accomplish on your own. Ask God for the wisdom and strength to move forward. Remember the great rewards that will come from your efforts.

- *Plan steps*: Create a plan. In what order do you need to take each step?
- *Action items*: How will these efforts keep you moving toward your goal?
- *Move forward in faith*: Is there any step you are afraid to take? How can God and the Holy Spirit help you overcome this fear?

DISAPPOINTMENT

You have discovered your life mission and are moving toward your destiny. However, be prepared. God will provide motivation and resources for you to do His work, but you will also face challenges along the way. The challenge may come just as you are making good progress and have achieved an important victory. It may seem like you have no "step" in your plan to overcome the challenge. It may seem like this obstacle is right in the middle of your path and stops all your progress. You might even wonder if you heard God correctly in the first place. You might ask, "Am I pursuing the right mission?"

Do not worry! You are not alone, and sometimes this can actually be part of the process.

Consider the story of Joseph in Genesis 37. As a young man, Joseph had two dreams in which God showed him images of his family bowing down to him. After having these dreams, Joseph began to experience problem after problem. He was dropped into a pit, sold by his brothers, falsely accused by Potiphar's wife, and thrown into prison. How Joseph must have doubted his dreams would ever come true!

Pastor Robert Morris explains Joseph's experiences in his book *From Dream to Destiny*. He shows that Joseph went through many years of testing and refining that built hope, perseverance, character, and faith. Joseph needed all of these tools to achieve his life mission: saving the lives of not only his family but also the people of Egypt and other nations.

David is another example of a simple man called to an extraordinary life mission. He probably had no idea what his destiny would be when Samuel first singled him out among the sons of Jesse. Imagine how David must have felt when the prophet anointed him as king!

Many years passed before David actually reached the place God prepared for him. During this waiting period, he endured continuous trials, such as fighting the giant Goliath, serving the emotionally unstable King Saul, and running for his life as the king tried to kill him. David spent years in exile, hiding in the mountains and caves. Bands of homeless men began to follow him; they could already see his destiny, even if he could not.

David must have thought his life mission would never be achieved, but it was during these years of difficulty that he developed the strength, courage, and group of mighty warriors he would eventually need to accomplish truly great things. God called David "a man after my own heart" (Acts 13:22), and although he was not without fault, today we think of David as a fearless shepherd, a skilled songwriter, and a God-fearing king.

Your life mission may seem impossible to achieve. Your current circumstances may try to convince you that your destiny is only a dream and perhaps it was wrong to pursue it in the first place. Don't believe this lie! Just as in the lives of Joseph and David, the challenges and obstacles you face—no matter how serious—are part of the process to strengthen and shape you into the person God wants you to be. Keep the faith. In God's timing, you can and will achieve the goals set for your life mission. It will not be easy, but when trials come, draw strength from those who have gone before you.

> Therefore, since we are surrounded by such a great cloud of witnesses, let us throw off everything that hinders and the sin that so easily entangles. And let us run with perseverance the race marked out for us, fixing our eyes on Jesus, the pioneer and perfecter of faith. For the joy set before him he endured the cross, scorning its shame, and sat down at the right hand of the throne of God. Consider him who endured such opposition from sinners, so that you will not grow weary and lose heart (Hebrews 12:1–3).

DON'T GIVE UP

When you begin a road trip, the scenery does not immediately change. However, after driving for a while, you will look out the window and notice things around you have changed.

Our life journeys are very similar. When we first make the decision to pursue our life mission and begin traveling toward it, we often see few instant results. This lack of change can easily frustrate us, in part because the modern world teaches us to expect results immediately.

Don't allow yourself to give up. It takes time to achieve anything great. Remind yourself what you have learned about your identity and the gifts God has provided to help you achieve your destiny.

Jesus was fully human and fully God. His two natures were in perfect union and perfectly equipped to accomplish His destiny. When you submit your life to Jesus, He gives you your identity and joins your will with His to create your destiny. Through the power of the Holy Spirit, you have the ability to fulfill your unique life mission.

As you move forward in faith, remember:

- Every day is a new day to start fresh.
- The unknown is only unknown until you take the first step. Fear can stop you completely, so you must choose not to be afraid.
- Create "I Am" statements. Your adversary, the devil, will try to tell you who you are. Remind yourself what God says about you.
- Check your progress regularly. Learn from the missteps and celebrate the wins.
- Check in with your accountability partner.
- Keep moving forward.
- Think about how the circumstances in your life affect what you do.

Now that you know your identity and destiny, ask yourself these questions once again. Compare your answers to how you responded at the beginning of this journey.

- Who am I?
- What do I value?
- What are my short-term and long-term goals?
- What would I be willing to die for?
- How is my soul today?
- Do I understand my giftedness?
- What is "the one thing" that would stop the hunger?

So do not throw away your confidence; it will be richly rewarded. You need to persevere so that when you have done the will of God, you will receive what he has promised. For,

"In just a little while,
    He who is coming will come
    and will not delay."

And,

"But my righteous one will live by faith.
    And I take no pleasure
    in the one who shrinks back" (Hebrews 10:35–38).

I thank my God every time I remember you. In all my prayers for all of you, I always pray with joy because of your partnership in the gospel from the first day until now, being confident of this, that he who began a good work in you will carry it on to completion until the day of Christ Jesus (Philippians 1:3–6).

Not that I have already attained, or am already perfected; but I press on, that I may lay hold of that for which Christ Jesus has also laid hold of me. Brethren, I do not count myself to have apprehended; but one thing *I do*, forgetting those things which are behind and reaching forward to those things which are ahead, I press toward the goal for the prize of the upward call of God in Christ Jesus (Philippians 3:12–14 NKJV).

For Christ did not send me to baptize, but to preach the gospel, not with wisdom of words, lest the cross of Christ should be made of no effect (1 Corinthians 1:17 NKJV).

"It's like a man who takes a trip, leaving home and putting his servants in charge, each assigned a task, and commanding the gatekeeper to stand watch" (Mark 13:34 MSG).

If any of you lacks wisdom, let him ask of God, who gives to all liberally and without reproach, and it will be given to him. But let him ask in faith, with no doubting, for he who doubts is like a wave of the sea driven and tossed by the wind (James 1:5 NKJV).

"The Spirit of the Lord *is* upon Me,

Because He has anointed Me

To preach the gospel to *the* poor;

He has sent Me to heal the brokenhearted,

To proclaim liberty to *the* captives

And recovery of sight to *the* blind,

To set at liberty those who are oppressed;

To proclaim the acceptable year of the Lord" (Luke 4:18–19 NKJV).

ENCOURAGEMENT

Who God wants to be for me right now,
the challenge that God wants to respond to in my life,
is who I get to become next.

—Graham Cooke

This is the beginning of a new day. This day is mine to use as I will.
When tomorrow comes, this day will be gone forever. I can waste it,
or I can make something of it. So what I do today is important;
I am exchanging a day of my life for it. I want to fill this day with
kindness and not cruelty; gain and not loss; good not evil;
purpose not meandering, so when it is over,
I do not regret the price I paid for it.

—Unknown

About the Authors

ALLAN KELSEY

Originally from South Africa, Pastor Allan Kelsey came to the United States on a swimming scholarship. He has been a believer since 1985 and loves engaging in meaningful worship, finding hidden truths in the Bible, and hearing from God. Allan is married to Stephanie—a Nebraska Cornhusker—and they have two daughters. Together, Allan and Stephanie have been serving Gateway Church ever since they moved to the Dallas/Fort Worth Metroplex in 2007. Allan is obsessed with helping people find their undiscovered potential. He loves watching believers learn who they are and how powerfully they are equipped to make unique contributions to this world. It is Allan's great joy to amplify this talent potential as the executive senior pastor of Human Resources and Strategic Planning at Gateway Church.

BRAD STAHL

With over 28 years of ministry experience, Pastor Brad Stahl has served as an evangelism instructor, itinerate speaker, youth pastor, children's pastor, administrative pastor, campus pastor, and Bible College professor. Brad graduated from New Life Bible College in Cleveland, Tennessee, in 1983, after which he traveled around America and ministered with the New Life Drama Company for five years. He has served on staff at churches in Australia, South Carolina, Michigan, and Texas. Regardless of location, Brad's constant desire has always been to find the treasure inside people. His passion and years of ministry experience have developed his ability to help people identify their special gifts and talents and find their place to serve others.

Brad and his wife, Dawn, have been married over 30 years and enjoy traveling, hiking, and exploring new places. Their greatest joy, however, is spending time as a family with their adult son, Eric. Brad joined the staff of Gateway Church in June 2006 and is currently the executive pastor of Staff Development and SERVE.